Buck & Tangee

A Love Story ... Sort of

Jon Zech

Copyright © 2012 by Jon Zech

Cover design by Jon Zech and Joe Ponepinto

Woodward Press, LLC, a Limited Liability Company
48929 Sugarbush
Chesterfield MI 48047

woodwardpress.com

All rights reserved.

ISBN-13: 978-0-9838261-9-4

For my wife, LaRue
(No, she's not Tangee. Really.)

Also great thanks to my writer friends who have helped so much. Especially Joe Ponepinto who has helped me herd this pile of words to completion, Christine Purcell for her encouragement and good advice, and to Stewart Sternberg for screaming obscenities at me when I failed to listen to said good advice.

Chapter 1	PlastiQueen	1
Chapter 2	Road Trip	35
Chapter 3	Things That Happened	143

Chapter One:
PlastiQueen

"A lemon holder?" I asked.

"For holding lemons. It keeps them from bumping into each other and keeps them nice."

Tangee showed me the picture in the PlastiQueen Party Catalogue of the flat, flying saucer shaped, pale yellow, lemon holder. She was being nice—she wanted money.

"It was just thirteen dollars and forty-six cents, including a dollar and thirty-six cents for shipping and handling. I can pick it up at Francine's any time after next Thursday."

"If you got to pick it up from Francine's, what's the dollar thirty-six shipping and handling charge for?"

"For getting it to Francine's, you dumb nut. What do you think, the post office is just going to take it to her house for nothing?"

I'd had experience with that kind of question before and avoided asking why, if a dollar thirty-six could get it to Francine's house, it couldn't get it to ours. A dollar thirty-six seemed kind of high, anyway. I looked over Tangee's copy of the order form and sure enough, right there below, "Lemon Caddie, Number 136-533Y, Daffodil Yellow, 1 @ 12.10," was, "$1.36 S and H." Just for a second I wondered why a yellow lemon caddie would be called "daffodil yellow." I also wondered at the other thirteen things on the list. And then I wondered at the two hundred forty-two dollar total price. Which included the twenty-one dollars it was going to cost us to send the stuff to Francine's house.

"You got an egg caddie, too," I said.

"It's for deviled eggs. It's got a top and a bottom and its own little handle. You make your deviled eggs and you just put them in here," she pointed to its picture, "and then you put on its little lid with its little handle and away you go."

"To where?" I asked.

"To where?"

"To where are you taking all those deviled eggs?"

"To a party or a picnic or wherever. And when I get there I just snap off the lid and the bottom turns into a deviled egg server. I'd just use it all the time."

"Why couldn't you put your deviled eggs in the lemon caddie and use that? They look about the same to me."

"Because there's lemons in the lemon caddie, you dumb nut."

"Silly me."

"Silly you."

I thought for a minute.

"Tangee?"

"Huh?"

"I've never seen you make deviled eggs."

"I didn't ever know how. But Francine says she has a recipe she's going to give me."

"And I don't remember the last time we bought more than one lemon," I said.

"Well, I never had a proper lemon caddie before, did I? Nut."

"Still, doesn't two hundred forty-two dollars seem like a lot of money?"

"It's a whole lot less than you'd pay in the store."

I restrained myself from saying that it was about two hundred forty-two dollars more than I'd pay anywhere.

"Besides, Bucky, it's fun. PlastiQueen parties are fun and everything looks so good, and if you buy enough you get a free gift. I got this little thing that slices butter into perfect little patties."

"We use margarine," I said.

"Same idea."

"Tangee, we use margarine in a tub."

"Not anymore."

I must have sighed or groaned or something, because she right away changed the subject.

"They got all kinds of parties, Bucky. There's PlastiQueen and DecorQueen...you remember when I went to that LaceQueen party—you didn't think I spent too much then."

She smiled and I remembered. Especially that little black lacy one-piece thing with all the hooks down the back. I never did get it completely unsnapped but at least it tore off real easy.

"And there's CandleQueen, too. That's the one I signed up for."

I gave her a look.

"It's for next week. If I do real good and sell lots of stuff I get to pick a free gift from the DecorQueen Porcelain Angel catalogue...anything up to page eight. And if I do really, really good, I could get to be an Associate Assistant District Representative. They make money from when they book parties and sign people up. A little extra money would be nice, wouldn't it?"

"An extra two hundred and forty-two dollars would be just fine," I said.

"So, I got to get ready for next week. It'll be on Thursday. You think you could get the rollaway bed out of the living room by then? It's been there since June."

I moved the rollaway bed and trucked over some folding chairs from Becky James' house and borrowed the twenty-cup coffee maker from the Moose lodge. Tangee got a book from her sister, Camay, that showed how to make all these pretty little cakes and snacks. I got to squash the strawberries and whack carrots into little sticks.

On Thursday, after the first women started showing up, Tangee told me I ought to go change the oil in the Chevy or something. Which I did. I change my oil after every three thousand miles or three major fights with Tangee, whichever comes first. So far I haven't made it past twenty-five hundred miles.

After four quarts of Pennzoil and one quart of Budweiser I had to get in the house to use the bathroom. They were just finishing up. Helena Harper who I hadn't seen outside of her own yard for two years, was all excited and talking to Tangee's aunt Betsy about the beautiful, frosted, three color, intertwined, "Unity Candle of Love" she'd ordered and how happy she was that it was on special, today only, for forty-three dollars and fifty cents, plus three dollars shipping and handling. That was three dollars to have it shipped to our house and handled by Tangee.

Three weeks later the stuff arrived—boxes and boxes of it. Tangee popped open the boxes and started pulling out plastic bags, each with its own candle inside. She was half way through when Francine showed up and helped her sort the bags into piles and match piles with orders. They piled and matched until they got down to a half dozen bags that didn't seem to go with any order.

While they were sorting and matching, I was snooping. Francine had all her order slips and invoices and shipping orders all over the kitchen table. She also had her Deputy Regional Sales Manager book lying there open. I mostly wanted to see about that shipping and handling business, but I learned a lot more. Like that Helena's beautiful, frosted, three-color, intertwined, "Unity Candle of Love," for forty-three dollars, came from Mexico and had cost Francine eight dollars and twenty cents…*including* shipping and handling. And Francine was just a Deputy Regional Sales Distribution Manager. There were still three levels of Distributor above her, and they were all making money.

After Francine left I told Tangee what I'd seen, "Baby, there's some serious money in this party thing."

"I told you so." She grinned. "Look here at the angel I'm getting." She showed me in her angel catalog the fat faced, winking cherub holding a lollipop who would be sitting in my bathroom in four to six weeks.

I said, "That's all real nice. How much did those eight women wind up spending today? Altogether?"

"I don't remember, exactly, but Francine said it was a real good party. It went so good that I'm having a PlastiQueen party next week. Three of them bought enough to get a free gift. It was a tin candle snuffer thing."

"Well, how much did they have to spend to get that?" I asked.

"You got the free gift if you spent between three and four hundred dollars. I guess altogether it came to about twenty-five hundred dollars, maybe."

"So you get a fat baby angel and three women get a tin snuffer thing and Francine gets five hundred dollars. And there's three more distributors on top of her and they're all making money, too. There's very serious money in this." I smiled and Tangee seemed happy that I seemed happy.

I went out to sit in my lawn chair in the yard to think. After my third Marlboro I could feel an idea rubbing around inside my brain. When Tangee's dad was alive he used to say that ideas were like turds: most often it's best not to try too hard, but sometimes you just can't hold them back. In the time I knew him, he was mostly constipated. I walked back to the house.

"Tangee?" I asked, "Those women at your party...were they drinking?"

"No, Bucky, drinking isn't generally allowed at Queen parties."

"Hmm. We got any of those corn nuts left?" We did and I dumped a handful into my shirt pocket got a beer from the fridge in the garage and went back to my lawn chair to catch the last hour or so of summer sun.

I started being logical about Queen parties and beer and fat baby angels and money. It was all women. I'd never heard of men going to candle parties or decor parties or anything like that. Men don't like candles. Men don't like decor. Men like other stuff. Men like beer and tools and trucks and sports. BeerKing Parties. ToolKing parties. TruckKing parties. SportKing parties. Men's parties. With beer. And maybe a lovely assistant to demonstrate wrenches and fog lights. Maybe a lovely half dressed assistant. If I could figure out how to do it, I could be the main head honcho chief distributor and make a ton.

I needed help so I called Roy. He's got a real good head for business. Roy's also my twin brother. Actually he's my Siamese twin brother. We were joined with my left shoulder to his right until we were almost six months old. It wasn't that it was that serious of an operation and our dad, Eddie, wanted it done right away, but our mother wouldn't hear of it. She said it was God's will that we were born that way, and that was how it was going to stay.

Later on in life our cousins would all kid us, saying that she kept us like that so she could put us in a circus freak show and make a million dollars. When we were thirteen we asked our Aunt Jane about it. She said it wasn't a freak show that mother was holding out for, it was Life Magazine and that all she was asking for was ten thousand dollars for the rights to our story. As soon as it became clear that Life wasn't interested mother forgot about the God's will part of it and had the operation done.

We were named Elroy and Elbert. Mother thought it was both cute and commercial, should *Life* magazine have taken her up on her offer. Dad always called me Buck and my brother Roy, and I always thanked him for that. The odd thing is, and dumb as it sounds, even though we were identical Siamese twins, we don't look all that much alike. For one thing, my hair is a couple of shades darker than Roy's and I'm about an inch taller. Our faces look the same, but he's had his nose broken a couple of times and as soon as he was able, he grew a beard. His grades in school were better than mine, but we always scored the same on those standardized tests they give you. He joined Mensa when he was twenty-one and quit after a month. He told me not to bother...no babes in our local Mensa chapter. Roy went into the army and then to college. I got Tangee pregnant.

"You want me to come to a party?" Roy asked.

"Not exactly," I said. "Tangee's having a PlastiQueen party and I want you to watch it with me."

Roy wasn't very excited about coming, but I worked on him for a while and he agreed that if it wouldn't take too long he'd come. Tangee didn't think too much of the idea, either. She said she didn't think Francine would like guys hanging around because then the women seem shyer and don't buy as much. I reminded her about the two hundred and forty-two-dollar check I'd written and the two parties I'd let her have. We compromised. She would let me and Roy sit, half out of sight in the kitchen pretending to play cards. That was okay with me because I didn't want us to be in the way...I just wanted to see how it all worked.

Roy got to our house early and we set up in the kitchen pretending to play gin. Altogether there were twelve guests. Tangee's sister, Camay, was there and she brought a friend from work and that friend brought her sister. Helena was there and so was her neighbor Patti. Our niece, MayAnne, came with two of her friends and Milly from down the street came too. She's eighty-five and I figured she was just in it for the squashed strawberries. I didn't know the rest of them.

Tangee had chairs all in a half circle in front of the coffee table, which had been draped with a navy blue velvet cloth. The show was slick. Francine and Tangee were like a tag-team pair. One would be setting up a display for a plastic thing while the other said all the wonderful things you could do with it. Like the Chip and Dip System. There was a main bowl for the chips and sticking out of the top of it was a post and on top of the post was a little bowl for the dip. And there were individual bowls that people could hold. Each one had a dent right in it where you could put the dip. Pretty clever. I guess everything was pretty clever because they couldn't pass the order book around fast enough.

"How much are those things?" asked Roy.

I checked the catalog, "Twenty-seven fifty. Plus shipping and handling."

"Hmmm," said Roy.

And Tangee? She was a star. She just gushed over every plastic thing that hit that navy blue velvet. Her eyes would get big and she'd go on about the wonders of the Salad Saver and the No-Bruise Banana Rack. I could see the ladies conjuring up ideas of serving their husbands perfectly saved green salads and beautifully unbumped bananas. Every kind of thing Francine and Tangee put on that navy blue velvet got a round of oohs and ahs…and orders.

"Well?" I asked Roy.

"Guys wouldn't do like that," he said. "They wouldn't ooh and ah. They'd burp and laugh and cuss."

"And then they'd buy," I added.

"Maybe," said Roy.

"If it was guy stuff, they would. If there was free beer they would. They would if there was a lovely half dressed assistant telling them how manly they'd be if they bought some wrench or tent or stuffed deer head."

Roy smiled. "You know, I think they would, too. I think maybe you've got something here. But we don't have anything to sell, do we?"

"Not yet," I said. "We just have to keep our eyes open and when we get a chance to buy some stuff at a close-out or something, we buy it. Cheap. I've heard of lots of times there's unclaimed stuff left in depots and truck terminals. We just wait until we can get a bunch of tools or whatever for like two cents on the dollar, and we set up a party thing like this and we'll make a ton."

"I guess I'm in if we can find some decent stuff to sell, but I'm not sure."

"Just keep your eyes open," I said. "I can feel it. This is going to be big."

The thing about getting rich is that you've got to be patient. You've got to wait until the time is right. It's easiest if you just forget about it until opportunity knocks, which is what I did. Then, two months after I started being patient, Roy called.

"Buck, do you remember that bait shop down by the boat launch?"

"Yeah. Dirty little place. Wasn't it called Burn's Baits?"

"Yup. And that's what happened. It burned. Two nights ago. I heard about it on my scanner."

"So?" I asked.

"So, it didn't burn too much before the fire department got there, but the insurance company is writing Mike Burns a check and he's going to bulldoze the place and put up a Dairy-Squeeze. He's got all this fishing stuff and most of it isn't even scorched."

I grinned, "BaitKing?"

Roy said, "I was thinking more like FisherKing, unless you think that's too literary?"

"BaitKing, for sure," I said. Then I asked, "What's it going to cost us to do this?"

"I talked to Mike and he said he'll take two thousand dollars for everything. You have a thousand dollars?"

"Yeah. I bet I can find that much. Let's do it."

"Okay. I'll call Mike back. We can meet him at the shop tomorrow afternoon. If it still looks good to you, we'll do it."

The next day was cool and sunny with a real nice breeze blowing in off the water. The bait shop looked sad and gray with lots of smoke smudges on the cinder block walls. The whole place smelled of wet, charred wood, melted plastic and scorched worms. The roof had caved in over the back part of the store but there was a lot of good stuff in the storeroom and in the display cabinets. I fingered a price tag on a super deluxe graphite fishing rod autographed by a champion fisherman; it was eighty-six dollars.

"Yeah, I think two grand is fair," said Mike. "Shoot, the insurance company already paid me for the stuff once. They call it damaged, but it looks okay to me. I got no way to get rid of it quick except a dumpster so if you guys want it, we got a deal."

"Sounds good to me," I said. "Now, that's two thousand for everything, right?"

"Yup, the whole inventory. Not the display cases. I sold them to somebody else already."

Mike took our cashier's check and we signed a paper he had in his pocket. He said, "This is just so there's no misunderstandings. I get the money and you get all the stuff, right? Everything. And you haul it away."

"Right." We shook hands and we invited him to the Beer Bar to celebrate his getting screwed so bad. He passed on it but Roy and I went anyway.

Two days later, about noon I got a call from Roy. "Buck, I'm at the bait shop. You still got that dump truck at your work yard?"

"Yeah," I said.

"Bring it and get here like right now."

"I'm kind of in the middle of something right now," I said.

"You just get here and you get here now or we can kiss our two grand goodbye. I'll explain when you get here."

I hurried, but my dump truck hadn't been started since last winter and I had to drop a battery in it. An hour after his call I met Roy in the bait shop parking lot. We had company. There were about a half a dozen guys in work clothes gathered around Roy. There was also a bulldozer, a backhoe and a big cube van.

"What?" I said, as I jumped from the truck.

"We've got to get this stuff out of here today…right now…by noon."

"Why?"

"That paper we signed had some fine print. We've got until noon today to get our things out of the shop."

"I didn't see any date," I said.

Mike walked up, "Yeah, Buck, read the paper. It's in there. That's part of the deal. I'm ready to level this place and get started on my Dairy-Squeeze store." He nodded to the men and equipment, "They're getting paid as of noon, and if your things aren't out by then, they get dozed. It's part of the deal."

We started moving things into my truck and it filled up a whole lot faster that I might have expected. The problem was that we didn't have any boxes to pack things in and lots of the merchandise was loose in the display cases, including lots of fishing lures which I learned you don't want to pick up more than one of with your bare hands.

I called Tangee and had her go to the grocery store and pack as many boxes of different sizes as she could fit into her little Chevy and bring them over. We toted armloads of fishing poles and boxes of reels to the truck. We started placing them neatly in stacks, but the closer we got to noon, the faster we worked and the more the stacks turned into piles.

I begged Mike to give us until two o'clock. He let his workers go to lunch, told them to be back by one and said that was the deadline. When the dozer fired up at one-fifteen and we were mostly through.

"We got the good stuff, Roy," I said.

"Yeah, I think so," he said. "There's still some cases of fishing line and some other things, but we got the expensive rods and reels and all. There's even some room left in the truck."

"That's good," said Mike. "You need some more room. You still have to get that stuff out," and he pointed to some low green enameled cases. "My guy is taking the display cases and the bait coolers, but they have to be emptied. He won't take them full. It's part of the deal," and he patted his shirt pocket where he had the paper we had signed.

"Well, hell," I said, "let them get dozed then. You got your money and we got the stuff."

"Read the paper," said Mike. "You don't take your merchandise…all of your merchandise…by the time it says on the paper, you have to pay for the work crew time and the time it takes my guy to empty out the cases. Dozer guys cost a lot, Buck. I'll give you another half an hour, then the clock starts running."

The display cases weren't much of a problem; we just swept the remaining things into Tangee's boxes. The bait coolers were something else. There were two of them, each about the size of a large refrigerator lying on its side. Each cooler held three deep, steel trays, and each tray held about half a cubic yard of wet, black dirt. The wet, black dirt was full of wet, red worms. The trays were too heavy to lift. Mike looked at his watch.

"Your pick up, Roy. Back it up here." I picked up a shovel.

"Oh, no! It's brand new, Buck. I just got it washed."

"My truck's too full," I said, and I looked at my watch.

"Tangee," called Roy, "run over to that party store on the corner and get a box of big strong trash bags."

Roy backed his new, white F-150 up to the bait coolers and lined up a half a dozen big toilet paper boxes in the bed. Tangee came back and we double lined the boxes with trash bags. Then we started to shovel. The six bait trays just exactly filled the six toilet paper boxes.

We pulled out of the parking lot and headed to my house.

It took a lot longer to unload the trucks than it did to load them in the first place. Fishing line got tangled with the fishing poles and the fishhooks got tangled in everything. At least they were light. The trash bag-lined worm boxes were another matter. They must have weighed three hundred pounds each.

"We could get some more boxes and some more bags and just shovel the worm dirt out from the truck and onto the boxes on the garage floor," I suggested.

"I think I've done all the shoveling I'm going to do today," said Roy. He lowered the tailgate. "Here, we all get behind and push the boxes off the end."

"But the boxes…they're just cardboard…"

"It's okay," he said, "those are super strength trash bags. Come on, let's do it. I want to go wash my truck, take a long hot bath and not think about this whole mess until the weekend."

It actually worked. We scooted the boxes off the tail of the truck and onto a picnic bench and then skidded them off the bench and onto the floor. There was very little worm spillage.

Roy went home. Tangee and I took a shower and went to bed, the only bright spot in an otherwise crappy Monday.

Tuesday morning I talked to Roy on the phone and we decided to forget about BaitKing at least until the weekend, when he'd come over and we'd start outlining the project. The week was a very good, blue sky, hot sun kind of week and I got a lot done at work, and around the house, too.

Even though I hadn't planned on thinking about BaitKing, I still came up with some ideas. Roy came over at noon on Saturday and we sat at the kitchen table with a yellow legal pad and wrote down how we would set up our BaitKing party.

"How much do you guess we're going to make on this?" I asked.

"It depends," said Roy. "We don't even really know what we've got. I had planned on making notes on what we got out of the shop, but shoot, the way we were heaving stuff into the truck, I've really got no idea. I guess the first thing is, we need to make an inventory and separate the things. Then we can talk about how much to charge and how we're going to get guys to come."

I snapped the yellow legal pad to a clipboard and we headed out to the garage. It had been hot all week, but this was the hottest day yet. I twisted the handle and swung the garage door open.

"Oh, geez…" said Roy as he stumbled backwards. He regained his composure long enough to barf between the hollyhocks beside the garage. I chose to vomit next to the rose bush. We stayed sick for most of the next half hour and then sat in the middle of the front yard sipping water for a while.

"I guess," said Roy, "there's a pretty good reason they keep worms in a cooler."

I nodded. "Yeah. It must have been like a hundred degrees in the garage all week. What are we going to do?"

"I think we open the side garage door and let it air out a little more, and then we get the shovels. We can't leave it like that."

I wondered for a minute why we couldn't. Winter would be here in five or six months and after the worms froze, they wouldn't stink. But then I couldn't use the garage much and Tangee would be on me every day about it and would finally shovel the worms out herself and I'd feel guilty and besides, if we couldn't get in the garage we couldn't do our inventory and then we couldn't have our BaitKing sale. "No, I guess we can't," I said.

I got my dump truck and we shoveled until dark. I don't much like the idea of messing up the environment, but I figured the worms and the worm dirt were all organic, so when I dumped them in the field behind the K-Mart, I didn't feel so bad. If anybody had questioned me I was going to say I was delivering topsoil.

While I was dumping, Roy was hosing down the garage floor, and by the time I got back all I could smell was the gallon of pine scented disinfectant he had finished up with. I left the garage doors open all night and by the next morning the floor was clean and dry and still smelled like a freshly cleaned toilet, with just an occasional whiff of something a little more earthy. We started our inventory.

By Sunday afternoon we had two major piles, one pile of things too scorched or burned or tangled to use, and the other of things we could actually sell. We sorted the saleable stuff into categories, wrote down how many of each thing we had and what their price tags said. There was thirty-seven thousand dollars worth of fishing gear in my garage. BaitKing was looking up. We sat on my front porch sipping lemonade and began to brainstorm.

"I figure we start with about a dozen guys. That's how many people Tangee had at her last party and it went pretty well," I said.

"Maybe we should start smaller," said Roy. "You know, just with a few guys so we can get the hang of it and make sure they will really buy."

"Like a test market?"

"Yeah."

"I hate to waste our first shot on a small crowd," I said. "I think I'd rather jump right in. Guys will go nuts for this stuff. We can charge half price or even less and still make out. We feed them some beers and get them bragging about their fishing and they'll buy. And remember what I said about a lovely assistant?"

"The lovely half-dressed assistant?"

"Yup."

"How are we going to do that? I know your wife. Tangee will go nuts. Besides, I don't think there's a heading for 'lovely half-dressed assistants' in the phone book."

"We do it on Tangee's bingo night so she won't be home. And besides, she shooed me out of the house when she had her parties, so she won't be the least bit suspicious. And I bet we can find the lovely assistant real easy. We just go to Bob's Bar."

Bob's Bar used to be Smith and Son's Studebaker-Packard in the fifties. Then it was empty for a long while until, in the seventies, it became the City Lights Disco. Then it was a hall that catered to weddings and after that it was Cowboy Bob's Dance Hall. Now it's just Bob's, but under the newest ownership, they took down the words "Cowboy" and Dance Hall" from the outdoor sign and now there's an extra "O" in Bob's name and it's called a gentleman's club, and your wife better not know you go there.

Roy and I went on Tuesday night. After our eyes adjusted, we made our way to a back corner, ordered beers and checked the place out. Neither one of us had been there for several years. The music was newer and louder than I was used to and I had to lean close to Roy so he could hear me.

"Seems kind of quiet tonight," he said. "And I don't mean the music." He scanned the room. "Not much business."

He was right. There were fewer than a dozen guys at the various tables and booths. On the main stage was a girl, who if I'd seen her at the mall, I wouldn't have ever thought I'd see her at Bob's. All she was wearing was a g-string and a pair of wire rimmed glasses. She was quite small breasted and maybe ten pounds over skinny. Her dance was just a step, step, step, in time to the music and her face looked like she was mentally writing her grocery list for tomorrow. The music ended, she nodded to the three guys who clapped. She gathered her discarded clothes and a small towel from the floor and held them to her chest as she stepped off the main stage and over to a smaller one behind the bar. Another girl took the main stage, a new song started playing and they danced. Around the bar, the girls waiting their turns on the stage chatted with the guys or danced, topless, for them at their tables. That was different. When I'd been here before, the girls just danced on the stage and weren't even allowed to talk to customers.

"That one?" asked Roy nodding at the first dancer.

"I don't know," I said, "she doesn't look too interested in anything. We need somebody who might at least smile. We got stuff to sell."

We spent a few songs comparing the girls, their bodies and the relative promotional abilities of their smiles.

"Hi." It was a tall girl with long blonde hair who we hadn't seen yet.

"Ah, hi," I said, shyly. How is it possible to be shy in a place like this? Isn't this the most open place in the world? A man should be totally unshy here. But I wasn't. Roy talked to her for a minute and she sat down. I looked at the foam on my beer. She was wearing blue jean shorts and a short sleeve blouse that was completely unbuttoned, but mostly covered her. Maybe that's why I was shy. Here she is, and all of her friends, walking around mostly naked, and here we are, the guys, all covered with clothes. It was like I wanted to tell her, "Excuse me, miss, but your shirt seems to be open." I don't know.

I was glad Roy was doing the talking because I wouldn't have known what to say. He was discussing mortgage interest rates with her. She was buying a house and was wondering about the advantages of a thirty-year loan over a fifteen. She said to me, "What do you do?"

"I'm in construction," I said.

"Want me to dance for you?"

"Ah..."

"Yes, Mindy," said Roy, "he does." He took some bills out of his pocket and laid them on the table.

"Okay," she said. "There's a new song starting right now. Or did you want to wait?"

"Now's good," I said.

"Great. I love this song."

It was a slow song. She crawled up and knelt over my lap, rocking in time to the music. Her blouse slipped off both arms at the same time and she bent forward to kind of hover over me, her head beside mine. Then she whispered right next to my ear, but I couldn't quite catch what she said and was too surprised to say, "Huh?'

The four-minute song was over in twelve seconds and Mindy said, "Another?"

I didn't say no, and one more song later she stepped back. "I got to go up," she said. "I'll be back, later maybe?" She put on her blouse and walked away.

Roy had this quiet laugh on his face. "You haven't been here for a while, huh?"

I shook my head. "You think she'd do our party?" I asked.

"Too hot," said Roy. "We need somebody who will get the guys loose enough to buy our things. Fishing gear is the last thing on you mind right now, isn't it?" I nodded. "It'd be the same with them."

I agree and we spent the next few hours "interviewing" the rest of the girls at the club. About half of them thought we wanted to hire them as escorts. The rest just said they never dated customers. We were about ready to leave. So was the girl with glasses who we saw when we first got to the club.

She was wearing regular street clothes and carrying a duffel bag as she talked to the bouncer at the door. We were about to pass her on our way out when the bouncer must have said something funny. She laughed. She smiled. She was it. We asked to talk to her for a minute before she left. The bouncer gave us a hard stare, but she said okay and led us to one of the quieter tables.

In two quick sentences Roy explained that we were looking for a demonstrator for some merchandise we were selling. He told her she'd be like a model. He showed her a picture of his wife and kids and also his driver's license and swore it was all on the up and up. Her name was Molly but she went by the name of Desiré at the club. Molly was skeptical. I showed her pictures of Tangee and Fatboy, the dog. She agreed. We finalized details about money and got her number, telling her we'd call when the date was set.

We were ready to go when she said for us to give her our driver's licenses again. She took them to a back room and returned with the licenses and a photocopy of each one, which she gave to the bouncer. "Just in case," she said.

As we drove home I wondered if Mindy had left any stray blonde hairs on my shirt.

Roy and I sat in my driveway for the best part of an hour hashing out details of the party. He had a little pocket calendar and we decided it would happen two weeks from Saturday.

Roy and I have had our best talks at midnight sitting in a driveway. When we were teenagers Roy's clapped out twenty-year-old Chevy Nova was our ride, our clubhouse and our therapy couch. We talked about girls and jobs and other guys at school. Mostly it was about girls. We planned our two-week getaway to the hills of Tennessee when we'd camp and live off the land. Maybe we'd chop wood for some farmer and he'd give us a chicken. We talked about killing a chicken and how we'd do it and if we could do it at all. We just knew that right over the hill there would probably be a pair of girls, sisters maybe, who were from Connecticut or some other mysterious place, and they'd have come out here and they'd be living off the land too. They wouldn't have the heart to kill their chicken so we'd have to do it for them. And they'd be grateful. That driveway conversation lasted about two hours. The trip never happened, but that didn't stop those driveway moments. Now it seems we still find ourselves every few months yakking until midnight.

We both had to work at our jobs pretty steady for the next while and didn't get together again until the actual day of the BaitKing Party.

He got to my house at noon and we spent all afternoon getting ready for the party. Tangee said we ought to have balloons and streamers like she did for PlastiQueen, but I told her this was just for guys and they wouldn't care about those kinds of decorations. The only decoration they would care about was Molly, but Tangee didn't know about her.

I got all the chairs arranged like Tangee had had them, in a half circle around the coffee table. Then I remembered the navy velvet cloth they had used to set things on and I sent Roy to the fabric store. While he was gone I jammed as much beer as I could get into the refrigerator and made sure we had enough chips and salsa. I found myself wishing Tangee had bought the PlastiQueen chip and dip system, but figured paper plates would do. Roy came back from the fabric store without the navy velvet.

"Do you know how much that velvet costs? Unbelievable. I got this instead."

Roy unrolled about eight feet of green indoor-outdoor carpeting.

"See?" he said. "It's like grass. Better to sell fishing equipment from grass than velvet, don't you think? And when we're done I can put it on my deck."

We laid it on the coffee table and it looked okay but it wasn't very soft and didn't hang too well. It was six feet wide and stuck off the ends of the table.

"It'll work," I said.

We lugged merchandise in from the garage and stacked it on our side of the table, ready to open and display. We checked our homemade order book and then rummaged around looking for a working ballpoint pen. Tangee was being fussy.

"Now you know to have a separate page for each person?" she said.

"Yes, dear."

"And don't just hold things up. You have to pass them around so they can hold them. Francine says that's important to get them to touch things…that way they feel like it's almost theirs already."

"Yes, dear."

"And you can't just say here's this thing or that thing. You really have to talk about each thing and what it will do. The clients need to be excited."

I thought about Desiré and guessed being excited was the last thing we needed to worry about. Then I looked at my watch. I had to pick Desiré up in less than thirty minutes.

"I'll remember all that," I said. "It's about time for you to go to bingo." I smiled a little conspiratorial smile at her. "If they see you here they'd be afraid to spend too much, because you'd tell their wives. We'll be okay. What time were you supposed to pick up Camay?"

"Now, I guess. I better go," she looked hesitant. "You sure you boys will be all right?"

"Positive."

She puffed up two sofa pillows and turned an ashtray a quarter turn. Finally she left.

"What time will she be back?" asked Roy.

"I told her not before eleven. To give us time to clean up and all. Look, the guys should start getting here any time now. I'll go get Desiré and you finish up here and get beers for the guys when they show up."

I followed Roy's directions to Molly's place and pulled into the parking lot of a small, single story apartment block. She came to the door and squinted out at me. Then she took her glasses from her shirt pocket and put them on.

"Oh, hi. Come on in. Pardon the mess."

I didn't see much mess. A few toys on the floor and a Barney tee shirt across the back of a chair. Her two kids were eating popcorn on the sofa and a woman carried a laundry basket across the room.

"Mom, I told you not to worry about the laundry. I'll get it first thing in the morning."

"It's okay, hon. The kids have their movie and I'll just dump a load in while dinner's cooking."

"I'll be ready in a minute. You can wait in the kitchen, if you want."

I sipped a glass of ice water while she picked up the Barney shirt and toed the toys toward a toy filled cardboard box. She was wearing jeans, a white tee shirt and an open plaid blouse that flapped lightly as she walked. Her blonde hair wasn't natural but it wasn't harsh, either. It was soft with light curls that swayed in time to her walk. Her gold-framed glasses sparkled and when she smiled at one of the kids, she showed a lot of small white teeth.

She came into the kitchen with a bulging chartreuse duffel bag and thumped it on the floor. "Almost ready," she said, and scooted away. It was hard for me to realize that she was a stripper and I was picking her up for a job. We could have been going on a picnic.

"Okay," she called from the apartment door. "Would you get my bag?"

I hoisted the duffel bag and judged that it couldn't weigh less than thirty pounds. She hopped into my car and I tossed the bag in the back seat. She tilted her head and said, "Thank you." I felt tingly in my stomach.

"Your mom is watching your kids?" I asked.

"Yeah, she's good about that. Sometimes I have to work nights at the club and she comes over. Usually I work days so I can be home right after the kids get back from school. Sometimes nights. Sometimes jobs like this. Not very often."

The evening was settling in soft and warm. The sun balanced on the horizon and laid there all squashed and orange. As we drove the wind puffed her hair and it seemed like every strand had its own sparkle. She didn't seem to mind getting her hair puffed.

She said, "Did your brother tell you about how this is going to work?" I nodded. "Nobody touches me. Period. I just help you show the stuff you're going to sell. I wear a swimsuit. Then, after you're done selling and if I like the crowd, maybe if they feel generous, I might take off my top and do a few dances. Maybe. And my mom knows your name and address and if I don't call her every hour or so, she calls the police."

"There won't be any trouble," I said. "These are just regular guys."

"Regular guys can get pretty stupid with a few beers in them," she said. "Two of my friends went with some guys for a thing like this on their boat. They were just going to hang out and look pretty and maybe get half naked and dance. They were just regular guys too, but they got off shore a little ways and drank too much and all of a sudden they're treating my friends like they were hookers or something. It was a nasty couple of hours."

"Did they...?"

"No. The guys got all pissed off but they didn't force it. They could have. I don't work jobs like that."

We bumped into my driveway and I helped her with her bag. I took her to the extra bedroom, down the hall from the living room and showed her where the bathroom was.

"She's even pretty in the daylight," I told Roy.

He smiled, "Yeah, and she's a smart girl, too. She's been to a bunch of parties and the like, and she told me this sounded like a clever idea."

We made a few last minute attempts to arrange our fishing gear and recentered the indoor-outdoor carpet on the coffee table and set out an extra bowl of salsa. There was a rattling knock at the screen door.

"Harry! Come on in." Harry is my next door neighbor. I usually only see him on Saturdays when we mow our lawns. We have kind of an unofficial, unannounced contest to see who can finish first. "We've got lots of good stuff."

"I might get something for my nephew," he said. He spotted the chips and sat down.

The door rattled again and it was my friend Louis and some guy from his shop. Coming up the drive was Roy's mailman. Within twenty minutes we had eleven guys sitting and standing around the room, drinking beer and munching chips.

At eight o'clock I took a deep breath and stood up behind the coffee table. "Well," I said, 'it's real nice all you guys could come. This is the first BaitKing party ever and you're in for some real good deals. Everything we got is first class and we got it real cheap, so you're going to get stuff for like half of what it would cost you at the store."

"Is it guaranteed?" asked one of Roy's friends.

I hadn't thought about that. "Well, I guess if something is messed up when you buy it, we'd give you your money back. If it breaks or something while your using it, you'll probably have to call the manufacturer. But hey…for half price?"

"Now," said Roy, "we could just stand up here and let you look through this stuff, but that wouldn't be near as much fun as we got planned. We've got somebody to help us pass things around and just generally perk up the atmosphere. I'd like you to meet our lovely assistant, Desiré."

On her cue, she stepped out of the spare bedroom and stood next to Roy. She was wearing a bright, flower-printed wrap which hung from her hips, and over an orange, flower print bikini top she had on a thin white blouse, unbuttoned and tied at the waist.

I don't know if I expected the guys to go wild and cheer or to jump up and charge over to her or what, but when they just sat there looking at her, I was surprised. Roy said, "Guys, this is Desiré and she's going to help us show you what we've got."

After another quiet five or ten seconds Lenny said, "Hi, Desiré. Nice to meet you." Then everybody else smiled and said their hellos and we got started.

Roy said, "This is a brand new Bennett Model 622 graphite shaft fishing rod. It's got stainless steel fittings and a WearTex grip." He was reading from the manufacturer's tag attached to the rod. He flicked it a couple of times and handed it to Desiré. While she was passing it around, Roy announced, "And if you like that rod, just imagine how cool it would be with this…" and he held up a Martin Spin-O-Matic spinning reel. Desiré brought the rod back and Roy attached the reel, fumbling just for a second as he figured out how it worked. She must have noticed that John, sitting in the green folding chair was looking more at the rod than at her, so she took it over to him and let him handle it first.

"It's a real nice one, isn't it?" she asked him, putting her hand on his shoulder.

"Yeah." He swished it a few times, barely missing a lampshade with his back swing. "Feels real good."

"Hmmmm," said Desiré. "I bet it does."

"How much for this setup?" asked John.

"Well, you can see the tag," said Roy. "The rod just by itself is ninety-one dollars. And the reel is another sixty-five."

John said, "Oh," and Roy said, "But not today. This is a BaitKing party and today that whole setup is fifty-five bucks."

There was a general mumble of approval, and one guy said, "Dang, that's pretty good."

I got the sheet with John's name on it and said, "Put you down for one of them?"

"Yeah," said John. "Probably. Let's see what else you got."

"Yeah," said Lenny. "Let's see if you got any more beer, too."

"Wouldn't be a BaitKing party without beer," I said, and went to the kitchen to get a couple more six-packs.

Roy and Desiré showed fishing lures and fishing line and lead sinkers and aluminum nets. When they showed plastic worms, Desiré shrieked. When they showed plastic waders, Desiré took off her flower print wrap skirt and pulled them on. When they showed a multipocketed fishing vest, she took off her blouse and modeled it over her bikini top. She laughed and joked with the guys, and seemed to be having a good time. I wrote orders and brought beer. The more beer I brought, the more orders I wrote.

Finally we were out of merchandise to show. Roy and I sat down with the guys and Desiré. I opened a beer and said, "Well, that about does it. We'll add everything up and get your orders together and you'll have everything delivered to your houses by next Sunday. And there's no stupid shipping and handling charge, either."

"I bet there's one more thing we'd like to see," said Wally. He stood up, wobbling a bit, and fumbled in his pocket. He came up with a couple of twenty-dollar bills. "Come on, Desiré, show us them pretty lures you got there. Sit down with me and we can discuss my fishing rod." He patted the front of his pants.

Desiré had said that after we were done she might get a little naked, but really I hoped she wouldn't. It had just been a fun party, and she'd been pretty sexy all right, but nothing too bad. She didn't get a chance to answer.

"Wally," said John, "don't go getting all stupid. Sit down and shut up. This girl don't go in for that kind of stuff. She's a real model. She's got class. You ain't got no class."

Wally sat down.

We all finished the beers we were working on, and one at a time the guys left, shaking our hands and hugging Desiré at the door. It was getting close to the time Tangee would be home so Desiré gathered her things together in her bag and I lugged it to the car.

The night was clear and cool as I drove her home. "Roy's paid you already, right?"

"Yes."

"It was a good party. Thank you," I said. "It wasn't so bad was it?"

"No. Actually, I had a good time. I thought those guys would die when I put those fishing pants on."

"So, when we have another party, you'd come back?"

"Yeah, maybe. We'll see."

As I pulled into her parking lot I thanked her again and she said, "You know what? This was the first job like this I ever did where I didn't have to get naked or whisper bullshit in some guys ear or get groped or leave feeling like shit. I was a model. Like at the auto show or something, huh?"

"Yeah," I said. "Just like that."

"I always wanted to be a model."

I stopped the car. She said, "Good night, Buck," and then she leaned over and kissed me on the cheek. She reached in the back seat and swung her duffel bag like it weighed nothing. I called goodnight as she walked to her door. I'm sure she didn't hear me. I barely heard myself.

"Buck, you were right. This was a great idea." Roy sat at the kitchen table with the order slips.

"Got a total?" I asked.

"Thirty one hundred dollars is all."

I sat down. I rubbed my cheek. I said, "Huh?"

"Three thousand, one hundred dollars. Most of it we get when we deliver, but I've got over eight hundred in checks right here and about sixty in cash money. And the way it adds up we still have enough gear for three or four more parties."

"It really worked," I said. "Lots of things could have gone wrong, but it turned out perfect." Then Tangee came home.

"Over three thousand dollars," I told her.

"That's good," she said quietly, her eyes hopping around the room. "That's real good," she said walking slowly passed the sofa.

"And we cleaned up, didn't we?"

"That's good," she said staring at the ceiling.

"Thirty-one hundred dollars," I said again as she walked out of the living room. I looked at Roy. He shrugged. Tangee came back to the living room.

"I thought this was a guys only party," she said.

"It was," I said. "How many women you know that want to buy fishing gear?"

"At least one," said Tangee.

"I got to go," said Roy, heading out the door. "I'll stop by tomorrow and we can get the orders together. Okay?"

"Yeah," I said as the screen door slammed.

"So, who was she?" said Tangee, her arms folded and her eyes hot.

"Who was who?" I asked. Maybe if I confused her, I wouldn't have to lie.

"Who was the skinny little blonde with the green eyes? A stripper? A hooker? What?"

Lying gets complicated. Every part of a lie has to get backed up with another lie and then you have to remember every part and get it right the next time you have to repeat the lie. Also, when you finally get caught, you're in more trouble for the lie than you would have been for just the thing you're lying about. It's not worth the trouble, especially when the thing you're lying about isn't really so bad to begin with.

"A demonstrator," I said. "Roy found her." Okay, half a lie. "She was like a model. Like at the auto show."

"You got a fishing pole model? You got somebody to model bait? I don't think so. I think you got some kind of call girl to do things while your little party was going on. What? Did you get yourself a little bit of that model, too? What?"

"It wasn't like what you think. She really was just a demonstrator. In a bikini. Really. Nothing bad happened."

"Something happened bad enough that you would lie about it."

"I didn't lie."

"You would have. Or at least you sure weren't going to tell me about it, were you?"

"No. You would have got mad." I told her how it all went, from

Roy's finding her, to my picking her up, to her mother with the basket of laundry, to Wally being rude, up to me taking her home. I skipped the part about the kiss.

"That's all just fine," said Tangee, "except you're leaving out the part about the sex."

"There wasn't any of that," I said, wondering if there was any residual lipstick on my cheek. "How do you think you know all this stuff, anyway? Blonde and green eyes and little?"

"You think you're so smart, Buck Crimmins. I know some things, too."

That's the truth. Tangee is one of the smartest people I know, except the things she's smart about are things they don't test you for in school. She's not sure if Germany or England are in the United States. She firmly believes that mice can just happen if you leave a pile of old rags in the garage…like the rags cause the mice by some kind of magic. She also believes in magic. I think she knows that some of the tricks are just tricks, but she's also pretty sure that psychics can bend spoons with their brains and that lots of people can read minds. But she knows people. She can meet a couple for the first time and be with them for fifteen minutes and tell you which one's cheating on the other and how soon they will get divorced. She's right about eighty percent of the time. She knows things.

"So, how did you know?"

She walked over to the sofa and pinched up a long blonde hair. "Elegant Expressions Number 104, Natural Honey Blonde."

"Good grief. Green eyes…was that a guess?"

She held up a piece of Kleenex. "This was in the trash basket in the spare bedroom. It's eye shadow. A Natural Honey Blonde woman using this color of eye shadow has green eyes."

"How did you figure she was little?"

"There's a dent in the bedspread in the spare bedroom. Her butt is smaller than mine and she weighs less. About one oh five. Size two."

"Well, I've got to say, you got that all right on. All but the sex part…how do you think you know that?"

"Because you're men and she's a cute little blonde, that's how."

"Nothing happened. Nothing."

"Yeah, right," she said.

"Okay," I said, "Where did this sex happen? Figure out some clues about that. Where? In the bedroom? You think I could have cleaned it up so perfect that there's nothing left but a butt mark on the bed?"

"No. Men can't make a bed like that. It wasn't in there."

"In the living room?" I asked. Maybe I was getting too bold, but nothing had happened. "Like one of the guys did something with her right in front of everybody? Shoot, I know these guys and half of them can't even take a piss in a public urinal if there's a guy standing at the one next to them."

Tangee was quiet.

"Maybe in a car in the driveway? Maybe under the lilac bush? Can you see old Lenny under the lilac bush with some young skinny, green-eyed blonde? Get a flashlight and check for butt marks in the grass. It didn't happen in any of those places because it didn't happen."

The good thing is that women mostly want to believe their men. The problem is that mostly they can't, or at least they shouldn't. I have the advantage of not wanting to have sex with any woman except my wife. Really. And Tangee knows it, even when her senses tell her not to.

"You should have told me," she said.

"I guess."

"Thirty one hundred dollars?" she asked.

"Yup."

"Men are creeps," she said and she punched me on the shoulder. "I think it's bedtime. You can watch your car races while I shower."

I laid in bed with my arms folded behind my head and watched something on the sports channel that might have been lacrosse. I could hear Tangee singing Patsy Cline songs in the bathroom as she dried off, and that's always a good sign. Three minutes later she was snuggled up by my side.

"You know," she said, "actually it was pretty smart of you to get a demonstrator. That kind of thing wouldn't work with women, though."

"No, I'm pretty sure it wouldn't. Women might enjoy seeing some handsome guy at one of their parties, but they wouldn't buy any more because of him. Maybe less. I guess getting Molly was kind of clever."

"Molly? I thought you said her name was Desiré?"

Yeah, I did. That was the name she wanted to use. Her real name is Molly."

"Molly? Green eyes. Blonde hair. About a size two. Oh. Oh!"

"Oh?"

"Molly Camden. Two little kids?"

"Yes."

"Molly Camden. I know her. I know her," Tangee's voice was getting strained. "I've been to PlastiQueen parties with her."

"Oh?" I said carefully.

"But…she's nice. I know her. I know her. She was here? Tonight?"

"Yes."

Tangee rose up and slapped my shoulder, hard. Then she started slapping it hard with both hands.

"Molly Camden was here? In my house? Tonight? While I was gone? Oh, Buck, how could you do that to me!? Oh, no."

"I'm sorry. I didn't know you knew her. But honey, nothing happened."

"She was in the spare bedroom!"

"Believe me baby, nothing happened."

"But I didn't clean it! The bedroom. The mirror on the dresser, it's all dusty. And the trash can was half full. And everything! I didn't clean! She must think I'm such a pig, but it isn't my fault. I mean, we haven't used that room for a long time. I should have known. Bucky, you should have told me. Oh my God…did she use the bathroom?"

"Ah, maybe?"

"Oh, Buck, how could you have done this? How am I going to

face her if we see each other at a PlastiQueen party?"

I told her that maybe I was wrong and that she hadn't actually had to use the bathroom after all. I told her that we had rushed her out of the bedroom when the guys arrived and that she couldn't have been in there more than two minutes. I lied like crazy and kept lying until Tangee settled down a bit.

"You're going to have another fishing gear party," she said.

"Yeah, we plan to," I said. "But just guys. No women. No Molly. I promise."

"Oh, yes you will. You'll have a party and you'll have Molly Camden help you and you'll tell me at least a week ahead of time and I will scrub this house, every inch of it."

"I guess if I have to…"

"But maybe next time she could wear a tee shirt and shorts or something instead of a bikini?"

"That would be fine, dear."

I got up to get a drink of water and when I came back to bed Tangee was already mostly asleep, muttering to herself, "Got to dust the woodwork." I slept pretty well.

The next day Roy called and asked if I'd rather meet him at the donut shop. I told him it was okay and that he could come over, which he did, although he couldn't look Tangee in the eye. He breathed easier after she left for the store.

We got out the order sheets and went to the garage. Twelve guys had made orders so we made room for twelve piles on the floor.

"You think we ought to do it one guy at a time or one item at a time?" I asked. "Like, a bunch of them ordered that first fishing rod you showed. Should we get them all out and then go to the next thing?"

"Let's start with those rods," said Roy.

We pulled the rods from the back of the garage and put one in each of six areas.

"But, wait," I said, "Lenny got two of them."

"And John got three. And most of them ordered with the reels we showed. Get the reels."

"Okay, nine rods and what…six reels?"

"Seven. One guy just got the reel and a different rod."

"I think we've only got six. There's six in a case and we've only got one case."

"What about the one we used for demonstration? That makes seven."

I said, "I think that came from the case."

"Okay, okay, wait a minute. You were right. One pile at a time. We'll start with Lenny."

"Okay, for Lenny…two rods, one reel."

"Check."

In business, organization is the key.

It took over a half hour to pull Lenny's order. The glow-in-the-dark plastic worms had gotten mixed in the box with the plastic hopping crawdads. He had also ordered our Super Assortment of plastic bobbers, but when we located them we found that most of the small bright yellow ones had been melted in the fire into one giant faded yellow bobber. We made an executive decision and substituted extra medium red ones. We picked and piled and made check marks on his order sheet.

"Should we wrap his order now or do all the wrapping at the same time?" I asked.

"Wrap?" said Roy.

"Yeah. We can't just dump this stuff on his porch. Wouldn't be professional. PlastiQueen things each come in their own little box with foam popcorn inside," I said.

Roy asked, "What kind of box do you put a six foot fishing pole in?"

"They got cardboard mailing tubes down at the Box and Ship Store, but I think for a six footer we're looking at like five dollars apiece."

"How's this? We go to the grocery store and get a bunch of little boxes. We put the small things in them and leave the rods unwrapped."

I said, "I guess, but PlastiQueen stuff sure looks neat when it arrives. Every little box says 'PlastiQueen' right on it."

"Well," said Roy, "our stuff is going to say Lemon Pledge or Campbell's Chunky Chicken Soup on it. It doesn't matter. We finish the piles, then we go to the store and just get as many boxes as we need."

We went to the next order and that one took the best part of an hour because the Sharpie-Special Fish Hooks had some how gotten mixed up in the yellow fishing line. Also at one point we couldn't read my writing and had to guess as to which lures he wanted. We tossed in an extra orange one in case we had messed up.

By the end of the evening we found we had sold two more of the reels than we actually had, and that the medium, aluminum framed nets had burn holes in them. We also determined that the case of Duo-Flex Stainless Steel Spinners was actually a case of Mike's old Playboy magazines. This delayed our sorting for about an hour.

It turned out that with clever substitution and "bonus" items we could fill all of the orders, barely. We decided that after the guys looked at their purchases, if they were unhappy, we could toss in a few more bonuses or maybe even lower the price a bit. I wanted to finish the job but we couldn't get the boxes we needed for wrapping because by the time we'd pulled all twelve orders it was after nine o'clock at night and the store was closed. I threw a tarp over the piles and we went in the house.

Over dinner Tangee asked how the sorting went and volunteered a bit of advice. "You shouldn't have the next party before a month or two. That way you can invite new people and some of the old ones, too."

"I don't know if there's going to be a next party," I said. "We're pretty much out of rods and reels. There weren't near as many as we'd thought at first. What we have left is hooks and line and about two dozen Kiddie Fishing Kits. It's okay, though. We made over three thousand dollars, so that makes back what we have into the project and five hundred apiece besides."

"No more parties?" she asked.

"Probably not."

"Hmmm. Maybe I'll just have Molly Camden over for lunch one day. One day when you're at work."

Roy called that night. "You didn't cash any of those checks, did you?" he asked.

"No, I do my banking on Friday."

"Good. Lenny just called and had to cancel his order. We have to give him his check back."

"His whole order? It was over two hundred dollars. He could just give us a new check for the things he's keeping."

"That's the problem. He's not keeping any of it. His wife had a fit that he bought any of it."

"Okay. I'll pull his check." Tangee tapped me on the shoulder. "I have to go. John's here to pick his stuff up."

John hadn't even walked half way into the kitchen. He kept brushing his John Deere cap against his thigh. "Buck," he said, "I had a real good time at your party. I really did. But I spent way too much. Truth is, you guys did too good a job. Truth is, I haven't been fishing in twenty years, and I didn't care too much for it then. Truth is, I don't have enough in the bank for the check." He looked at the linoleum.

"It's okay," I said. "It was fun wasn't it? Shoot, it's enough that we had a good time." I got him his check. He handed me a twenty-dollar bill.

"It's for the beer," he said. "And the pretty girl. It was fun."

I put the money back in his hand and said, "John, you couldn't drink twenty dollars worth of beer in a month. Don't worry about it."

He left, still apologizing. Later that night I found he'd slipped the twenty under a Coke can on the kitchen table. By the following Wednesday every single BaitKing guest had backed out of his order. The married ones caught hell from their wives and the single ones realized they couldn't afford it. It turned out that John's twenty was the only money we made, period.

Thursday evening Roy and I rocked on the front porch and considered our next move. We were now two thousand dollars in the hole, plus the beer money and the two hundred dollars for Desiré.

"Want to give it another shot?" asked Roy.

"I think I'm tired of BaitKing," I said.

"Let's call Mike and see if we can sell him the stuff back. It's all sorted and cleaned. Maybe?"

We went in and called Mike. He wasn't interested. But he gave us the name of the guy who was the losing bidder on the merchandise. He said he had offered five hundred dollars, but we had out bid him.

"I didn't know we were bidding," I said.

"Yeah," said Mike. "You won." I took the losing bidder's name and number.

"Roy," I said, "we could have had this whole lot of stuff for maybe six hundred dollars."

"Oh. I thought I got us a pretty good deal."

Our daddy used to say, "It's not the deal you got that counts, it's the deal you think you got." Our daddy was a smart man.

I said, "Let's take the five hundred dollars, if we can get it." We had to deliver the fishing gear to the buyer, but he had five hundred dollars cash.

Two weeks later, Tangee had a PlastiQueen party. Molly Camden bought a hundred and fifty dollars worth of things. She told Tangee she thought our house was cute, and *so* clean. She acted like she'd never been through our doors before. I got home from work just as she was leaving. I nodded hello. She smiled goodbye. Her glasses sparkled.

Chapter Two
Roadtrip

There ought to be a thing like a snooze alarm on phones so when it rings you could just whack it once and they'd have to call back in ten minutes. I was pretty well into a mid-afternoon nap when the phone chirped. I tried to make it part of my dream but I woke up anyway. I wish I could have just whacked it so they'd call back. Tangee can just let it ring. She'll let them leave a message even when she's just sitting there doing find-a-word or watching her soaps.

I picked up the phone.

"Buck? It that you Buck?"

"Yeah, it's me, who's this?"

"Leonard. Leonard Pant. Buck, you've got to come down to the police station and bail me out."

"You're in jail, Leonard?"

"No, you ignorant SOB, I'm in the freaking dog pound…I'm Queen of the May at Knot's Berry Farm…yes, I'm in jail! Listen, Eleanor is in Ishpeming with her sister and Bob's at some plumbing convention in Buffalo and nobody else I know has got any cash and yours was the only number I could remember and I only got this here one phone call."

"So let me see if I've got this right. There's one guy within five hundred miles of here who can do you any good and you've just called him a son of a bitch. Is that about it?"

"Aw, Buck…"

"Now, just what do you think the chances are that that SOB is going to haul his ass off his nice warm couch and help you out?"

Leonard begged and pleaded and apologized and sounded for a minute like he might have been going to cry, so I hauled my ass off my nice warm couch and drove down to the jail. It was more than kindness. This was Saturday and it was poker night and without Leonard Pant there'd only be five of us. I put Leonard on my VISA and we left.

The first thing he said was, "Will you take me to the airport?"

This sounded suspiciously like my credit card was going to take a serious hit so I said, "Leonard, you're not going to the airport or the bus station or anywhere else. You're just going home. Besides, it's poker night."

"No," he said, "I just got to talk to the airport guy. He's the one had me arrested."

I said, "We've got to talk about this," so I made a right turn and drove us to the Beer Bar.

The Beer Bar used to be the Trophy Tavern but then they lost their liquor license after that problem with the topless dancer and her ferret and now all they can serve is beer and wine. You don't have to be male to go in but you've pretty much got to be a guy to stand it for very long. It's dark and there's lots of smoke and stale beer stink. And don't wear anything better than jeans because the old red plastic covered bar stools are cracking and curling and they'll snag you good if you wear anything fancy, like polyester for instance.

Once Emmett Brimley brought his wife down to the Beer Bar for their wedding anniversary. She must have thought they were going someplace else because she had on this short little black dress, nylons, spikey heels and a real mad look.

They sat through Emmett drinking three beers. The only entertainment that night was watching the plastic Miller HighLife girl twirl on the plastic Miller HighLife sign. Some nights there's a hard-boiled egg eating contest and once in a while a mouse race. There's also a TV but since nobody could agree on a station, Lucky set it on CNN Headline News and melted the channel changer button with his BIC. He also inadvertently melted the volume button to "real, real quiet." If everybody stops talking at the same time and the beer cooler motor shuts off, you can almost hear it real plain.

All through Emmett's three beers, his wife, whose name no one can remember, was talking at him. It was that kind of angry-wife-in-a-public-place talk; all hard eye-looks and little coded comments that only a husband would understand.

Emmett just watched the plastic Miller HighLife girl spin and blink. Then he burped. Real loud. His wife spun her head toward him so fast the black and red sequined comb flew out of her hair and landed in the popcorn.

She screeched one long screech of cusses at Emmett and lurched off the bar stool…but not too far. The red plastic upholstery snagged into her nylons and a splinter from the underside of the bar grabbed her dress. She also caught one of her spikey heels on the bar stool rung. She went down, her dress went up and the back of her nylons stretched out about three feet before snapping back and starting to unravel. She wasn't hurt but it was so quiet you could almost hear Wolf Blitzer on the TV. We never saw her again. Neither did Emmett. I wish I could remember her name.

So, Leonard and I walked into the Beer Bar and stood there waiting to get our bearings. Going into that place on a bright afternoon is a lot like when you take a tour of Mammoth Cave and they walk you around and show you all the stalac-things hanging down and the frozen waterfalls and the white crickets and then they stand you in the middle of this huge cave and turn out the lights and it's so dark you don't even know if you've got your eyes shut or not. After a few minutes we could make out the Coors sign behind the bar and headed that way. Lucky got us a couple of beers and a coffee filter full of popcorn and we took it over to a booth. I patted the seat checking for beer spillage and slid in.

"Buck," said Leonard, "Yesterday was the last day of winter. Today it's spring."

"Yeah?"

"Well, I don't know if you remember, but last fall I ran this promotion at the hardware store. I sold a ton of snow blowers because I gave everybody a money back guarantee. I said if it didn't snow at least twenty-four inches this winter I'd refund half price to anybody who'd bought one. It didn't seem like much of a risk 'cause we always get like three or four feet of snow."

"Not this year," I said.

"No. In fact as of last Monday we were at exactly nineteen and a half. But then this last storm came up. They were saying like six to eight inches of new snow, but the there was a high pressure system over Lake Michigan and an occluded frontal system was stuck over Manitoba and that messed things up. I've been watching the weather channel a lot. I've also been spending a lot of time at the airport."

"I wonder why they always say that?" I wondered.

"Say what?"

"Six to eight inches. Or four to six inches, or eight to ten inches. It's always even numbers. They never say, like, five to eight inches or seven to nine. It's always even numbers." I sipped my beer and thought about that for a minute.

"Buck, it doesn't matter. The point is they said there was going to be a lot of snow…or at least enough that I could get out from under that money-back thing. That's why I've been hanging around the airport. That's where they officially measure the snow and the rain and everything.

"There's this one guy out there, Orton Weeks, and every midnight he measures how much snow there's been for the day.

"I was at the airport at eleven o'clock last night." Leonard was leaning over the table and talking low. "I'd been checking snowfall at the hardware store all day and figured we'd had about five inches so far and it was going to be real near to my twenty-four inch guarantee by midnight, but it was going to be close and I wanted to be there to see. I usually brought an extra hot chocolate for Orton and he let me walk out to the collection box with him. Big airports got it all computerized, but Orton still has to check it by hand.

"About eleven-thirty, he's getting ready to go out to the box and then it really starts to snow…big old fluffy chunks of snow…it was piling up like crazy. I figure if he checks the box just a few minutes after midnight, like maybe ten after, then all these big fat snow flakes will put me over the top.

"So we're just walking out the door to check and I kind of stumbled and most of my hot chocolate sort of accidentally spilled onto Orton's left leg and down into his boot. He jumped around for a second, but it wasn't all that hot…just pretty sticky I guess. So he hopped over to his desk and pulled off the boot and peeled off the sock and rung it out and set it on the radiator. Meanwhile, I'm looking at my watch and it's five after midnight and I'm looking out the window and seeing flakes the size of Kennedy half-dollars just piling up. Then Orton sees what time it is and he cusses and puts his boot back on without a sock and heads out the door, cussing all the while as to how the box has to be checked right at midnight and giving me dirty looks."

In spite of myself I was interested, "So what was the reading?"

"Well, we get to the box, and he checks it and the gauge says five point five inches. That makes twenty-four and a half for the season…I'm in! Then Orton checks his watch and by now it's like quarter after and he takes off his glove and gives the box a little rap on the side. All those big flakes settled and the gauge reads four point seven…I was short by three tenths. Orton says, 'Got to adjust for the delay,' writes down four point seven and starts walking back.

"Oh, Buck, I begged the man. I said, 'Just write down what you first saw. It was five point five, come on Orton,' but he just kept on walking. I was desperate. I told him if he'd mark it at five point five I'd give him a hundred dollars."

"You offered the weatherman a bribe? How much money do you stand to lose with less that two feet of snow?"

"About forty thousand dollars."

"Well then, how come you offered such a pissy little bribe?"

"I was up to five hundred by the time we got back to his office and before he got his boots off I was at a thousand."

"That's more like it," I said.

"So he says, 'wait a minute,' and goes in the other room. I figure he's looking for dry socks. Turns out he called the police. That was last night. Then today I called you, and that's why I have to get out to the airport. I've got to talk to Orton and get him to drop the charges.

Walking out of the Beer Bar is as much of a challenge as walking in. We had to stand a full minute before we could even halfway open our eyes. The sun was so bright it hurt the backs of my eyeballs. By the time we got to the car I was still half-blind but we started toward the airport anyway.

We were there in half an hour and Leonard pointed me toward the main building that served as hanger, tower and meteorological station all in one. As soon as we walked in Orton saw us and flinched.

"Now Leonard," he started, "don't you go starting anything. You're in quite deep enough already. Interfering with a federal employee who was just doing his duty is right serious stuff."

Leonard held up his hands, "Orton, it's not like that. I just came to talk."

"I'm not dropping the charges Leonard."

"Well, it would be real nice if you would, but that's not why I'm here."

Orton looked suspicious of Leonard's intentions. So did I.

"You're not?"

"Nope."

"What, then?"

"The charges don't much bother me. It's that snow thing…the measurement you made." He looked at the floor. "It's going to break me. You know about the guarantee thing? That last half inch you didn't count, it's going to cost me forty thousand dollars. Can't you just go with the five and a half inches like you first measured?"

"No, I can't hardly do any such a thing. The measurement has already been reported. It was on the news. Four point seven is the number. And those charges better bother you. Really. You could be looking at…well a long time behind bars and a pretty hefty fine."

"No, I don't think so. Those charges won't stick. I didn't do anything wrong…not like you did."

"Bribery is plenty wrong, and what do you mean like I did?"

"I never offered you anything. You never heard me offer you anything. And more important, nobody else heard any such a thing either. I was just this fellow spending time with his lonely buddy. And as for you, you're the one who was late to his post to make his official federal observation and you're the one who made an 'adjustment' to make up for it. And then you felt guilty and blamed me for your being late.

"So, Orton, the way I see it, to make everything right, you've got to send a corrected reading showing five and a half inches…after all, that's what you first saw wasn't it?"

"I guess."

"And with that corrected report filed, I wouldn't have any reason to offer this so-called bribe, now would I? I think maybe you mistook my joking for a real offer."

Orton had a lot of conflicted looks crossing his face all at once, but mostly he looked scared. Reputation meant a lot to him, being a federal officer and all.

"I think," said Leonard, "we'd all look a whole lot better if you just called in that it was a typo in your report and it was really, say, five point seven instead of four point seven."

"What about the police?" asked Orton.

"Well, you could just tell them that you've slept on it and realized that maybe you misunderstood and overreacted and that now you see how it actually could have been just a stupid little joke on my part. You could even say that, 'a stupid little joke,' and I wouldn't mind that you said my joke was stupid. They'd respect you for coming forward and setting a situation right…two situations, really, counting the snow measurement mistake and all."

It was just that simple, too. Orton made two phone calls in five minutes. He explained about the stupid little joke to Officer Billy Bark at the police station and that he wanted to drop the charges and Bark just said, "Okay." The other call he made was over his computer and that went even faster, just click, make correction, click, send. That was all. Leonard and Orton shook hands, and between the two of them, Orton looked to be the more relieved.

Leonard and I drove back toward the police station to get his bond cancelled and my VISA card recharged. After that Leonard offered to buy me a burger, but I turned him down. Drama like that gets to be exhausting.

"I can still get in some decent nap time if I drop you off now," I said. "We're still getting together to play cards on Saturday, aren't we?"

"Well, yeah. Now that I'm not out that forty thousand, I'll be there. It's at Mink's house this week isn't it?"

"Yup. Seven-thirty."

The guys like it when we play cards at Mink's house. His wife is a real good cook and sometimes she'll fry up a ton or so of kielbasa with onions and peppers. Tangee means well but last time we played at our house she made creamed chipped beef on toast and a big bowl of butter beans. It tasted good but it's not exactly poker food.

I got home and Tangee wasn't there yet so I plopped my butt back to where it was on the couch before Leonard called and pretty soon I was asleep.

Late afternoon naps aren't nearly as satisfying as early ones, especially in the winter. I think a nap by definition ought to happen when the sun is still out. Otherwise it's not a nap, it's just sleeping. Also, later in the day there are often fewer sports on the TV that are good to nap to. Sometimes you're stuck with football, which is bad because even a crummy football game is interesting, so the best I can manage is a light doze. Bowling is a good nap sport and in the summer so is golf. Just a nice low background sound, no plot and not too much crowd noise. I was lucky that afternoon and found a Canadian station showing the regional curling quarterfinals. I got in a good forty minutes.

A few hours later I was seated at Mink's kitchen table, sipping beer and riding out a steady loosing streak. I was down eight dollars.

"Whose deal?" asked Scuddy.

"Who cares?" said Leonard Pant. He rubbed the edge of one of his few remaining chips against his cheek.

I hadn't been paying attention, "Me, I guess. Five-card stud. Ante up."

"Geez, Buck, that's all you ever deal," said Louis.

"Don't whine, Louis," I said. "Ante up."

All I deal is five-card stud because it's easy. Some of the games the guys come up with get pretty complicated and I don't think gambling should take all that much effort. Mink likes a game he calls, "Nine card cross-over, roll your own, match-up." It involves all these cards laid out on the table and each player gets three more and you have to match your hand with some of the ones already dealt. But only if they're spades or they total nine. Or something. I dealt and peeked at my down card, a seven. Then I started dealing the first up card.

"A ten for Leonard," I called, "Mink gets a deuce, a queen for Scuddy, a nine for Rusty, a ten for Louis and dealer gets a jack. Queen bets."

Scuddy has the most expressive face I've ever seen and usually that's not a good thing when you're playing poker, but the thing is, he's *always* expressive. It's like all of his thoughts are directly connected to his face muscles. He had a big old grin on his face as he looked at his hand but that could mean anything from him being already paired up with aces to him having severe gas or that he just remembered his aunt's phone number. You never know. He clattered a red twenty-five cent chip onto the ante pile. We all followed.

"Shoot," said Rusty, "in Vegas they'd laugh their ass off at the thought of ten cent chips and ten dollar pots. Vegas is something."

"When were you in Vegas?" Scuddy asked.

"Ten, twelve years ago. That time I was going to marry Juanita." Rusty leaned back in his chair and stretched his legs. "We went out to get married but by the first afternoon she'd lost all of our money on roulette. And I mean *all* of our money. We didn't even have enough for any kind of ceremony or anything. Just as well. She'd spent everything but the fifty dollar bill I keep tucked in my wallet for emergencies."

"That sounds like an emergency to me," I said.

"Yeah. It was a package thing and our plane home wasn't leaving for three more days. We made out okay eating on the cheap and walking around a lot. There's a lot of free stuff to see."

"Is it beautiful?" asked Mink. "Like on TV?"

"Yeah," said Rusty fondly, looking up at the ceiling fan. "And there's women there, too. Tons of women. If I hadn't been with Juanita…"

"I always wanted to go," said Leonard. "It's just that every time I was ready, something came up. I've been to the casinos in Detroit."

Rusty laughed. "Only thing that's the same is the color of the felt on the blackjack tables. Vegas is… well, it's just something else. I'd love to go back. Without Juanita."

"So let's go," said Mink.

"Huh? It's time to go home? What?" said Scuddy, suddenly dazed.

"No. To Vegas. Let's go. The six of us."

We all talked for about five minutes about how great it would be, but then Leonard said he thought the cheapest package flight would be about six hundred dollars.

"Yeah," said Rusty, "and then you've got to figure on rental cars and food and shows and women. It could add up."

"Well," said Mink, "what if we drove?"

"No," said Leonard Pant, "twice a month poker with you guys is plenty for me. I'll be damned if I'll spend two weeks with the five of you jammed into Louis' Buick."

"What about my motor home?" said Mink. "We could fix it up and take that."

"No, we couldn't," said Leonard, "because you don't have a motor home."

"I've got the bus."

I'd forgotten about the bus. About five years ago Mink had bought an old sixty passenger Bluebird school bus and it had been lying dead in his backyard ever since.

Mink said, "I'd always planned on fixing it up into a motor home, but I'd just never gotten around to it. It wouldn't cost much if we all chipped in and worked on it together. I'd pay for materials and we'd split the work. Six guys chipping in on gas would be a whole lot cheaper than six package airplane trips."

We dealt a few more hands of poker but nobody was thinking much about cards. As soon as we finished up Mrs. Mink's snacks, we put on our coats and went out to see the bus.

It was up on blocks. "I've got the tires in the garage and a couple times a year I jump start the motor," said Mink as we crunched through the snow to the garage. The Blue Bird was close against the side of the garage with a few inches of hard March snow drifted around the concrete blocks it rested on. In the light of a half moon, a sixty-watt bulb and two flashlights it looked like a giant, frozen block of Velveeta cheese with a black racing stripe. Mink had already stripped out the passenger seats leaving only one for the driver. The back of the bus was as hollow as an empty beer can, but didn't smell as good. Some odd chucks of two by four and a small roll of carpet were stacked against the rear emergency door. Something scurried.

"There's livestock in here," said Rusty.

"A couple of mice, I guess," said Mink. "I figured as long as I wasn't using it, they could. I'll put out some traps or something."

It wasn't exactly a deluxe motor coach. We walked back to the house and nobody said much.

Finally Mink said, "Once we get it cleaned out and you see it in the daytime and we get it fixed up, it'll be nice. I've been camping in a motor home. It's fun. I rented a thirty-four-foot Sylvan Aggressor a few years ago. And the Blue Bird's a lot bigger."

We agreed to meet back at Mink's house the next morning, Sunday.

I got there by ten o'clock and sat having coffee with Mink and Mrs. Mink. Louis showed up at eleven but it took until noon for all six of us to be there. The sky was gray and a drizzly little rain ran off the frozen ground and puddled in the snow. We stood in the empty bus.

"Damn, it's damp in here," said Rusty.

"That's because we aren't working," said Leonard Pant. "Let's at least get this thing swept out."

We had two push brooms, and two dustpans to work with. In three minutes the air was thick and Mink was coughing. "This dust is terrible," he said.

"It's dust and spider webs and mouse turds," said Rusty. "This crap could kill us."

We opened the side door and the rear emergency door to get some cross ventilation. "Now it's damp and cold," said Mink.

"Sweep," said Louis.

We swept and got probably three pounds of dirt off the floor and onto Minks back yard, where it belonged.

That only took an hour or so but Rusty figured it was time for a beer break. We hadn't brought any and Mink only had a few bottles in his fridge so Rusty, Scuddy, Louis and Leonard Pant headed over to the Beer Bar to recharge for the afternoon shift.

Mink said, "Think we'll see them any more today?"

"Nope," I said. "Not until next weekend."

"So, what should we do?" asked Mink. "It's swept out. Everybody but us is gone. What's next?"

I said, "I guess we'd better lay out a plan for what we're going to put in there and where it goes."

Mink and I sat at his kitchen table for the best part of the next hour, doodling floor plans and not getting too far. We had sketched a plan of the bus floor and cut out little cardboard shapes representing chairs and beds. Nothing fit right.

"What do most motor homes look like inside?" I asked.

"I'm not sure," said Mink. "I only rented that one and I don't exactly remember. But I do know they fit together a whole lot better than this." He nudged a cardboard chair out of the cardboard bathroom.

"There's a recreational vehicle sales lot down past the airport, isn't there? How about we go down there and look around at campers and motor homes and see what they're supposed to look like. Maybe tomorrow after work?"

Mink agreed and I picked him up the following afternoon. "I asked the other guys if they wanted to come, but they were all busy," I told Mink as we drove to the dealership.

The folks there were happy to let us into all of their models and even gave us shiny brochures for each one. The best one was the Redwood Avenger. It had seating up front and beds behind, with lots of storage space. It had a three hundred-horse power engine, air conditioning, a trash compactor, two waterbeds and satellite TV. It cost four hundred and ninety-thousand dollars.

"You know," said Mink, "for four hundred and ninety-thousand dollars a person could stay in the best hotel anywhere in the country for a thousand nights. I don't think I have a thousand vacation days left for my whole life. And six miles to a gallon…that could really add up. But, I guess there aren't always a lot of fancy hotels in places where you could drive the motor home. You could camp in your Sylvan Aggressor right in the middle of the woods."

"Sure was deluxe, though," I added. "Really much nicer than the Virgin Forest Probe or the Backwoods Penetrator."

We drove back to Mink's house and spent the rest of the evening copying parts of the Aggressor's floor plan onto our bus sketch until it looked like something we could live with. Then we made a list of materials we'd need. Since I'm in construction and get a discount at Builders Acres, I agreed to pick up our supplies.

I called Mink the next morning and asked him to come to Builder's Acres and give me a hand, but he said he's slept funny the night before and had a kink in his back. I didn't want to go alone so I asked Tangee to come with me. By the time she'd finished ironing, talking to her Momma and her sister, Camay, for a while, it was past noon before we got on the road.

We were driving south on M-25 and it was real warm for late March. I had my window half way down and the oldies station was in the middle of forty in a row. The hits just kept on coming.

Tangee was saying, "…and when you're through building your bus, we can take my Momma to Cowboy Rex's Western Pantry for dinner. She loves it there."

"Okay," I said.

"You do so like it," she said.

"I didn't say I didn't like it. I like the chicken there real well."

"Well, momma loves it and we should take her there. We have a car and can get around. She's stuck at home most all of the time. You can put up with it for one dinner."

"Okay," I said.

Tangee stared out the side window, "That's better. Besides, you like the chicken there, don't you?"

"Yup. But it's going to take me a while to get all the materials and take them over to Mink's and unload them. Then I've got some measurements to do and maybe get started on the carpet. It's twelve thirty. I'm thinking I'll get done around seven. Maybe we should get something to eat now."

"Can we stop at Sooper-Dooper Burger?"

"Sure. There's one right next to the oil change place by Builders Acres."

Tangee was singing along, first with Sam Cooke and then the Platters as we turned right onto Edward Murk Drive. The little strip malls were separated only by their parking lots and the occasional used car place. The red, white and blue Sooper-Dooper Burger sign leaned toward the street with its animated Sooper-Dooper Man pointing to the drive-through entrance. I pulled in and after several minutes we had edged up to the speaker and placed our order.

"Kravitz Henny Youngman boulder swell?" it squawked.

I said, "Huh?"

Tangee said, "She wants to know if you want anything else?"

"No," I shouted at the speaker. "I just want what I just ordered."

"Cleveland?" asked the speaker.

Not taking any chances I repeated, "Two fries, two Cokes and two Sooper-Dooper burgers, one of them with no tomato."

"Or onion," added Tangee.

"Or onion," I called.

"Kiss an elf," the speaker crackled.

I turned to Tangee, "Huh?"

"Six dollars and twelve cents and drive up to the first window and have a Sooper-Dooper day," translated Tangee.

"She said all that?"

"Just drive up."

It was lunchtime and the drive-up line wasn't going anywhere. I managed to squeeze about eighteen inches closer to the car in front of me. Over my left shoulder the speaker squealed, "Banned in Boston corn cob fritter anyway?"

I yelled back, "I can't move up yet…I'm still the same guy."

"Jean Paul Sartre," said the speaker.

"Right," I said, moving up another foot.

"Freaking jerk," said the speaker.

The line moved. Slowly. Hotel California started and ended on the radio and we were half way through the theme from Shaft before we reached the first window. I gave a sad-faced woman with pudgy hands a ten-dollar bill and hoped for the best in change. I got the bills all right but some pennies and maybe a dime fell to the pavement. "Oh," she said.

"It's okay, don't worry about it," I said as her window slid shut. She took my advice and didn't seem too worried.

We got our food and turned right onto M-25.

"I don't know why we go to that place," I said.

Tangee asked, "You want me to make up your Dooper Burger so you can eat it?"

She does this thing with the aluminum foil burger wrapper that's a combination of architecture and origami. It gives you your burger in a kind of shiny metal paper hand puppet with cuffs. It's a real skill and I bet she could get a patent on it if she tried.

Builder's Acres covers four acres. They have little maps at the door so you can find your way around. Tangee went off to look at lamps. They didn't have an aisle labelled Bus Parts so I aimed my flatbed shopping cart toward the area marked Interiors.

After the Carpet Salon and the Flooring Studio I got to Panel Land. The choice there was easy; I bought the cheapest they had.

Then I doubled back to the Carpet Salon. The Amazon Gold Shag looked nice but not very practical. We weren't taking a vacuum cleaner. There were Berbers and sculptured piles, some of them costing enough to bust our budget with just a few yards. Without any of the guys to consult, I decided to be economical, practical and stylish. I picked the green Astro-turf. It worked fine for my BaitKing display table, I figured it would work fine as a bus floor. Two young guys helped me measure the carpet as we peeled it off its giant roll and we scrunched it into my big cart, next to the paneling. Then I went to find Tangee.

She wasn't in the lamp department. I wasn't surprised. I pushed my cart over to the side of the aisle and sat down on my roll of Astro-turf. Builder's Acres covers one hundred and seventy five thousand square feet. Tangee covers one square foot. I figured she was just shopping around and would come back shortly. We had agreed to meet in lamps. After fifteen minutes I guessed that she'd not only gone shopping, but maybe she'd also had to use the bathroom. After a half an hour I wondered if she'd gone shopping, used the bathroom and met a friend. After forty-five minutes I knew that she'd gone shopping, used the bathroom, met a friend and been hit in the head by a stack of falling lumber. I left lamps to have her paged. On the way to the service center I spotted her sitting at a dinette table in the Kitchen Korner talking to her Momma on her cell phone. I told her that I thought we were supposed to meet in lamps but she said there was no place to sit there and she knew I'd find her when I went to have her paged. She finished her conversation and helped me push my cart to the checkout. Then she told me she'd be in the car, dialed her sister's number and walked out.

I stood in line a long time behind a young couple with stars in their eyes and wallpaper in their cart.

"I'm just so excited that we found this perfect Periwinkle Blue paper for the breakfast nook," said the starry eyed girl.

"Nook," said the starry eyed guy with a funny look on his face. Newlyweds.

"You!" said the girl, bumping him with a shoulder. He grinned and copped a quick feel as they jostled.

I wanted to tell them about the first rule of marriage. Whether you've been married two months or twenty years, *never* put up wallpaper together. Never, ever. Even if it means that the job takes three times as long. Even if it means the job never gets done. Sadly, as important as the first rule is, you just can't tell a young couple about it. They'd never believe you. Not until they'd done it themselves for the first time.

"No," she will hiss, "up. More up."

"I am moving it up," he'll say through clenched teeth from the top rung of the stepladder. "This is sure as hell up where I come from."

"That's too far," she will say. "The point of the third green leaf has to match the base of the bottom petal of the smallest blue flower."

"The third flower? There are a thousand freaking blue flowers on this damn thing."

"You swore at me," she'll cry.

"The paste is drying," he'll yell.

It will go on like that until one of them leaves the room. I wanted to tell them but they'd already paid and were jointly pushing the cart toward the exit, playfully bumping their hips with every step.

I put the carpet, the paneling and the other materials on my charge card and drove to Mink's house, dropping Tangee off at home along the way. I unloaded the two by fours and the paneling and all the other stuff into Mink's garage and decided not to be upset that I had to do it by myself. I also decided not to think about the project too much until the next weekend when we were all supposed to get together and start building.

That didn't exactly happen.

The next weekend came and I worked a few hours on the bus doing some additional cleaning and measuring. I cleaned and measured alone.

During poker that night I said, "You guys are going to help with the bus, aren't you?" I got a lot of, "Oh, sures," and, "I've been busies," but the next day it was just me working until about one thirty.

I had gotten the carpet cut to size and hauled it in the bus. I figured the carpet had to go in first before we built in the storage and everything. I was getting ready to get something to eat when Rusty showed up just at the same time Mink and Mrs. Mink pulled in the driveway. I told them they could take over.

"Well," said Mink, "Actually we just stopped off home for a minute. We have to go to my sister-in-law's house for dinner."

Rusty said, "Yeah, I thought I'd stop off and see how things were going. You guys haven't got too much done yet, huh?"

"Us guys," I said, "is me. How about as long as you're here you help me glue down the carpet?"

"If I was going to be working, I would have worn work clothes," said Rusty.

"When you work in them they'll be work clothes. Come on."

Between the two of us we were able to jockey the carpet into position. "Okay," I said, "I'm going to go. All you have to do is roll up the edges and squirt some adhesive down and then roll it back. Are you going to be here next Saturday?"

"Sure." Rusty sounded hurt. I left and went home. I ate a baloney sandwich and helped Tangee rake the winter junk out of the ditch.

I decided not to work on the bus the next Saturday. Rusty decided the same thing and didn't even show up for poker. Sunday morning I got to Mink's garage at the same time as Louis and Leonard Pant and Scuddy. The carpet hadn't been glued. It had been painted. Outside the bus door was a paint tray, a half-empty quart of white latex, a roller and some large paper stencils. We looked inside and found that Rusty had converted our green outdoor carpet into a football field. There were yard line stripes, hash marks and numbers. There were also half a dozen empty beer bottles. Most of the lines were straight.

It actually looked pretty neat. I just wished he would have glued the carpet down, too.

"Why do you suppose he painted a picture of a turd in the middle of the football field?" asked Louis. I looked and right at the fifty yard line was a white painted oval and in the oval was a brown painted blotch.

"Maybe it's not a turd," I said. "I think it looks more like a map of Cuba. See that dot up there would be Havana."

"No," said Leonard Pant. "Havana would be down here. Look, stand over here and squint your eyes. That's not Havana, that's an eye. It's a critter. Damn. I think he painted a picture of a mink."

We looked and squinted and figured Leonard was right and we agreed that it was quite an accomplishment for a half-drunk guy with nothing but a paint roller to work with.

The four of us glued and stretched and squared the carpet. Louis said, "I wonder if this is the kind of glue people sniff to get high?"

"No," said Scuddy, "that's airplane glue…the kind you use to put model planes together with. This stuff can't do that."

"Then I wonder…" began Louis, looking definitely unsteady, "…why it is that I'm about to pass out?" He took two little steps and leaned against the driver's seat. Then he sat down on the floor. He sat down hard.

We opened both the side and the rear door and helped Louis outside. Once he got a few breaths he was okay. None of the rest of us felt funny or light-headed so we blamed it on the tacos Louis said he'd had for breakfast. Common sense says that you don't have to go to the hospital for an upset stomach, so we let Louis air out for a while and went back to work.

With the carpet done and Louis more or less back to normal, we spent the rest of the day framing the storage area in the bus with two by fours and cutting paneling to size. By late afternoon Louis was feeling better and said he had a taste for Greek food and everybody left to find dinner. I went home.

That was the last day the majority of us were working at any one time. From then on it was either me alone, or me with one other guy.

Work was slow, but it was getting done. By me. Early in May I decided I was due for a weekend off. I skipped working on the bus and I skipped poker. I even skipped going to work until Sunday afternoon.

Foto-a-rama had ordered twenty-two of my eight by twelve model BC-9 buildings for drive-through coffee shops and I hadn't even ordered the materials yet. I figured I'd go to my office, write the order and fax it to the lumberyard.

The sign by the gate said, "Crimmins' Construction: World Headquarters – Buck Crimmins Owner and President." I make little buildings, and not just portable toilets either, although that was mostly what I made in the beginning.

So, that's what I do. I build little buildings, none of them more than eight feet wide. I make mobile construction trailer offices and photo drop off buildings and security guardhouses. I also still make portable toilets, but I'm getting out of that line. My real dream is to someday make a little house people could live in. Cities could buy a bunch of eight by twenty houses and just roll them to where the homeless people are. They'd be pre-wired, pre-plumbed and everything…ready to hook up and move in. I'm still working on the drawings.

I went to work the rest of the week and in my spare time I made drawings of my little house. They all looked like the bus. I went back to Mink's house Saturday morning and got back to work.

For the next few weeks I got some now-and-then help from the guys and the work went along. Somebody had to do it.

Mink had the clever idea of making the beds by hinging a piece of plywood to the bus wall for each of the beds. Then, when we weren't using them, we'd just swing them up out of the way and latch them to the walls. He also came up with some really smart storage cabinets with racks and magnets holding the doors closed and everything.

All that was left was the seating. We had agreed that each of us would bring a seat for themselves. I got a neat old recliner from the used furniture store. To get it in we had to fully recline it and push it through the emergency door tilted on its side. Mink got a front bucket seat from an eighty-four Bonneville out of the scrap yard and Louis found an armed, swivel desk chair. Scuddy still hadn't come up with his and we hadn't seen Rusty for a while but rumor had it that he was trying to borrow one of the stools from The Beer Bar.

We planned on leaving the last week of June.

We finished the bus about two o'clock on the day after Memorial Day. The five of us sat on the grass beside Mink's garage, drinking beer and admiring our work. A simple, beat up, nineteen eighty-one Bluebird school bus had become a simple, beat up, nineteen eighty-one Bluebird school bus with some cots and chairs and a Coleman stove. We were proud. Each of us walked through it again, scuffing at the new, football field carpet and patting the foam padded cots. We touched the smooth Builder's Acres, Washed Oak paneling. We admired the roll-up curtains Mrs. Mink had made out of some discarded, woven bamboo, yard sale, placemats. Slick. Rusty had finally come up with his chair. Actually, he brought two chairs. One was an aluminum and plastic chaise lounge, suitable for back yard tanning, and the other a tall, black vinyl barstool with an adjustable height mechanism. The Beer Bar wouldn't let him have one of their's.

I said, "Scuddy, where's your chair?"

He said, "Don't need one."

"It's a long way to stand," I said.

"I can't go," he said, looking down and kicking dust.

"How come?"

"Just can't"

I didn't want to ask if he was short of money. Rusty said, "Money?"

"Yeah."

"How short are you?" I asked.

"All short," said Scuddy. "I'm broke. My sister needed some money. It's okay. Next time, right?"

We had all done a fair amount of scraping to come up with the money for the trip and there just wasn't any to spare.

"We could make the trip one day shorter," Said Mink. "That would save money."

"Broke is broke," said Scuddy. "I couldn't afford it if it was one day or two days or any days less."

"No. I mean we could cut the trip by a day or so and that would make it cost less for each of us and we could give that to you. Besides, you've already paid for your part of the gas."

"We've planned this for a long time and I'm not going to take even one day away from your trip. I can't go. And…" he hesitated, "I got to ask for my gas money back, too. I'm sorry."

I was sorry too. Scuddy had known for weeks that he wouldn't have the money, but he kept working on the bus as much as anybody else did. I asked him privately if I couldn't take out a cash advance on my credit card for him. He could pay me back. He smiled and said thanks, but no. He just walked over to his car, waved goodbye and left.

It was only a week before we planned on hitting the road and Tangee was getting nervous. There's very little crime in our neighborhood, but that never stopped her from worrying about it. I tried to convince her that she wasn't going to be in any danger while I was gone, but she was being argumentative.

"What about the dog door? Robbers could come in through the dog door," she said.

"We've had that dog door for six years and no robber's come through it yet."

"But I'm going to be alone and that'd be just the time they'd come."

"Tangee, Fatboy can hardly fit through it himself. You're going to worry about a dog door that's almost too small for the dog?" Fatboy quit licking himself long enough to look up when he heard his name. He's mostly a cross between a Beagle and a fifty-pound sack of wet rice.

Tangee started ticking off her arguments on her fingers. "A raccoon could come in. A possum could come in. A *snake* could come in." Tangee hates all of those things, snakes especially. "And a robber could *too* come in through there. A robber would be skinny."

"He would?"

"Yes, he would. If he was fat, he wouldn't need to be a robber because he'd have plenty of food. He'd be skinny and he'd be homeless and he'd kill Fatboy and rape me and steal our stuff."

"A skinny, homeless, horny, dog hater who needs an eight year old VCR with a missing remote?"

"Uh huh, and he could, too, fit through that door. You look." Tangee went over to the doorwall that lead to the back deck and got down on her hands and knees in front of the built in plastic door-flap. "You watch. If I was a robber I'd do just like this," and while she was down on all fours she pushed the dog door out with her hand and poked her head out.

"Okay, but that's just your head."

"You watch." She backed up, straightened her arms in front of her like a diver and pushed through, her head and shoulders following. "See," she called from half outside.

"Not even half," I said.

She pushed and tried to get further but certain parts of her looked like they might get pretty smushed going through that hole so I got down by her and did some creative fondling.

"Buck! Not now!"

"I'm just trying to help, Mrs. Robber." I fondled a little more and finally her chest made it to the other side. Her hips were a whole other matter.

"Bucky…I'm stuck."

"Yup." I grinned and patted her butt. "Must be that Big Mac you ate yesterday," I said and patted her butt again.

"I'm coming back in, and you're going to get it," she said and started backing up.

I stepped out to the deck through the open doorwall and started to fondle her back through the flap, but it didn't work the same this time and she yelped.

"What happened?" I asked.

"I don't know. I'm too big to get back the way I came out."

"Your tits didn't get any bigger since we started this. Did they? Wouldn't that be something? We'd be rich. A magic dog door. Just crawl through it and you go from a 34B to a 36C."

"Bucky, don't joke. I'm stuck and I don't like this."

I had to be careful…I'd never get her out if she started crying.

"It's my shirt," she said, "it's got all bunched up."

"Okay." I unbuttoned her blouse and hung it over the back of a lawn chair. She was still stuck. "Well," I said, "I guess this is next," and I snapped her bra strap.

"No Bucky – what if Jim or Eleanor go in their back yard? They'll see me."

"Seems like we're short on choices."

It was one of those bras that open in the front, the ones that make you stop and think…is it bend and lift, or lift and bend, and for all that is it a right bend or a left bend? And anyway I tried it, it took both hands and my full attention, but I finally got it off and hung it next to her blouse on the lawn chair.

She tugged a few more times and said, "Okay."

Without all that fabric in the way she tried again, wiggling and bucking and arching but all it did was to turn her tummy red. I tried for a minute to figure out how to work this into some kind of foreplay at some future date, but Tangee saw the look in my eye and reached out to swat me.

She looked like pretty soon she might start to think about crying and I said, "Hang on, I've got an idea." I came back a few minutes later with an armload of stuff.

She said, "Huh?" and I held up a can of E-Zee-Cook Super No-Stick Frying Pan Spray. She said, "Ooh, no…" but by then I had the cap off and was half way through a nice even first coat across her back and was heading for her chest. She scrunched her eyes closed and said, "It's cold!" After I finished she rocked back and forth a few times and said, "I'll be here forever."

I said, "So, at dinner times I'll have to put a plate out here for you?"

"Please, Bucky, can't you just take the door apart?"

"I can if I have to. Let's try this first. Which one you want, Mazola Oil or Crisco?"

"Crisco – Mazola will drip on the deck. No, wait, I think Crisco is animal fat and Mazola is corn oil – I think corn oil is better for you. Or maybe it's the other way round. Or neither."

I got down on my knees on the deck and rubbed her down good. Then I put my hands on her shoulders and said, "Now you hold your neck real straight, I'm going to push your shoulders with my hands and your head with my stomach."

We were rocking back and forth like that and not getting anywhere. Just then, Jim and Eleanor stepped out onto their back deck. Tangee shrieked and that shriek must have squashed out all the air out of her lungs because with one more lunge she popped back through the hole slicker than a spit out watermelon seed. She sat on the kitchen floor all naked and greasy and red and wide-eyed.

We showered off the Mazola oil until the hot water ran cold. It was nice. Then we took a nap.

When we woke up Tangee said, "Bucky? You'll fix the door? So nobody can come in?"

"Yup. I'll cut a piece of steel that'll slide right over the hole at night."

"Okay. I'm sorry I get so scared. Not when you're here, but when you're not here. Sometimes I hear a noise and it's probably the dog or the wind or something, but I get scared."

"Your sister is going to be here while I'm gone, isn't she?"

"Not the same."

"Well," I said. "This make you feel any better?" I reached under the bed and pulled out my four-ten shotgun. "You just scream and show the end with the hole in it to a robber and he'll go away. Fast."

She seemed satisfied with that, and I didn't mention that I didn't have any shells for the gun.

The next day I cut a piece of steel to make a very slick, armored dog door. Then I had to do the grocery shopping for the trip.

*

People always gripe about getting the grocery cart with the shaky wheel. I look at it as more of a challenge. I just wheel it over to the household hardware aisle and get a can of WD-40. Usually all it takes is a quick spray and it's not shaky any more. Sometimes it takes more serious repairs. If they sell automotive stuff they sometimes have little wrenches and pliers, and I use them. It embarrasses Tangee if she's with me when I've got a basket half apart in the dog food aisle, but what the heck, the cart needed fixing and I'm not charging the store for my services. Most of the carts at my local store are in pretty good shape now.

I don't usually take Tangee grocery shopping with me. She has a hard time making choices so we wind up with both the chocolate nutty bars *with* coconut and the chocolate nutty bars *without*. She doesn't like the ones with coconut but she wouldn't want to offend someone who happened to stop by for coffee that had a preference for it. I don't care for either one and if I'm the one doing the shopping that's what I get…neither one. I just buy the stuff we usually eat and maybe a bag of Chips Ahoy. This Sunday we were shopping together.

I had a pretty good list of things the guys wanted to make sure we had in our bus pantry. I'd gotten the crackers and the canned chili and the beer. Louis wanted Spam. He had specified Spam, not any old store brand, blended, processed meat-like product, or the other Spam-like thing they call "Meet." He said Meet was a lot like Spam, but that it had a lot more of those little white lumps in it. I got the Spam. Most everything else we would need would have to be bought fresh when we needed it, since most of the refrigerator space would be taken up by beer. Rusty had reminded me that we needed beer-vegetables, so we were in the pickles, olives and other condiments aisle. All good beer-vegetables. Tangee was looking at mustard. She held a squeeze bottle of brown mustard for a long time, just looking at the label.

"I wish I would have thought of this eighteen years ago," she said.
"Brown mustard?" I asked.
"You know Maryanne?"
"Yes, dear. Our niece? That Maryanne?"

"You know I was the one who suggested that her name be Maryanne. If I would have thought about this when she was born, this would have been her name."

"Mustard Crimmins?"

"No, you nut, DiJon. DiJon Crimmins. That would have been such a pretty name. Don't you think?"

"I'm kind of used to Maryanne."

Besides the stuff for the trip we wound up with bok choy and endive and that funny brown mustard with specks in it and a pint of whipping cream and a pack of foot long hotdogs and a bunch of other stuff I didn't see her put in the cart. When we got to the checkout line she was still putting things in the cart as fast as I was putting things on the conveyor. I don't argue. It's just easier to buy it. She waited in the car while I hoisted bags into the trunk.

As I started to back out she said, "Isn't this just something?"

"Hmm?"

She rustled her copy of the American Galaxy Examiner Newspaper and held up the front page to show me the headline and its main photo.

"Okay," I started, "what's 'The Letter That Will Change The World.'"

"It's a miracle. They found a letter over in the Holy Land. It's a letter from Jesus Christ, Himself."

"A letter from Jesus?"

"Don't you go getting all that way," she said. "It says right here that it's a letter from Jesus, and they found it in this here clay jar right in his tomb. I'll read what it says and then I'll tell you all about it."

While she read the story to herself I had a real unholy thought. I'd always just figured Jesus couldn't read or write. Way back then hardly anybody could and there weren't any bible stories about Jesus in school or anything. I had imagined that if He could have done his own writing, He wouldn't have had to have His friends do it for Him. Then I remembered that He was a teacher, so it kind of made sense.

She finished reading just as we got home and she told me about the Jesus letter as we put the food away.

"Did they mention," I asked, "how it was that they managed to *not* find this letter before now? I mean that cave where Jesus rose from…it's not all that big and it's probably one of the most looked at rooms in the world. Don't you think somebody might have noticed this clay jar before now?"

"It was behind this rock," she said, "or maybe under it…they don't exactly say. It was a tourist who found it. She was from Michigan too." She rustled the paper. "Here, it says, '…found by twenty-two year old Lynette Foxnart of Columbus County Michigan.'"

I had to find space on the pantry shelf for three new kinds of pickles. "Who was the letter to?"

She grinned, "That's about the best part…you'll never guess. Go on, guess."

"Ah…Caesar?"

"Nope."

"Pharaoh?"

"Nope."

"His mother?"

"No, silly."

"Who then?" I jammed the speckly mustard behind the pickles.

"John Fitzgerald Kennedy, that's who."

"Jesus Christ wrote a letter to John Kennedy?"

"Yes, He did, plain as anything. It was a warning."

"So, it was like, 'Dear John. Sell the convertible. Love, Jesus.'"

"No. You make me so mad sometimes. No, it wasn't like that. He warned him about Castro. He said, '…and you better watch out for…' no, wait, I better read it." Tangee found the paper jammed into one of the grocery bags and unfolded it, brushing off a leaf of squashed bok choy. "Here. 'Bewarest thou of him from the South, he of the beard and the single banner.'"

"And this was written to John F. Kennedy?"

"It was written to J. F. K. but that's just the same thing. Well, it says it was addressed to F. J. K. but it's about the same thing except that they didn't have 'Js' back then so it was F. X. K. It's right here…look." She rapped at the cover photo with a stalk of celery.

I looked. There were maybe two-dozen little fragments of parchment or vellum or papyrus or whatever all laid out in a row, like a jigsaw puzzle where none of the edges quite matched. I shook my head.

"Why can't you believe Bucky? Wouldn't it be wonderful?"

"Yup, it would," I agreed. "But, baby, if it was for real it would be just like the headline says…it would change the world. And it might have been on Channel Seven Action News last night too. And on the front page of a real paper."

"It's not?" She seemed real sad.

"No, it's not. I don't think your pastor's going to be preaching about it tomorrow, either."

"It's a lie, huh?"

"I bet."

"Monday," said Tangee, "I'm going to drive over to channel seven and ask them. Maybe they're just not Christians down there and they want to cover it up. You draw me a map. I'm going down there Monday."

"I'll be on the road with the guys by Monday," I said.

"That's why I need the map."

When she has a plan she's happy. She put the Examiner on top of the refrigerator for safe keeping until Monday.

The day before we left I packed my clothes. One suitcase and one duffel bag held everything. Tangee helped by doing the socks and underwear count and made sure I didn't forget the lucky tee shirt her momma had bought for me—the one with the cartoon hand rolling dice. Below the cartoon was printed, "This Pair o' Dice is Paradise." She had also made a last minute run to the local dollar store to pick up a wide variety of tiny toiletries and some plastic containers for soap and my toothbrush.

At seven o'clock the next morning I carried my luggage out to my car. I came back in to say goodbye to Tangee and found her vacuuming the carpet. She looked up briefly as she worked and gave me a kiss. Over the roar of the Hoover she called, "Have a fun time, Bucky." I walked out to the car looking at the cloudless sky and felt funny. She hadn't even turned off the Hoover.

I backed down the driveway and glanced forward in time to see Tangee running toward me. I knew I hadn't forgotten anything. She wrenched open my door and practically dragged me out.

We kissed so hard we nearly fell over. "I didn't want you to see me cry. I didn't want you to see me cry," she cried in my ear.

"I know," I said.

"But I don't care," she said, and we kissed some more. "I *do* want you to see me cry," she whispered. "That's how you know I love you."

"You know I know," I said, hugging her close.

We kissed again, and she let go of me. "You be careful," she called as I got back in the car.

I mouthed an I love you through the windshield and blew her a kiss, but she'd already taken her cell phone out of her back pocket and was dialing a number. The lump in my throat only lasted a few miles. Okay, several miles. Okay, all the way to Mink's house.

I got to the bus and for once everybody was on time. We hooked up Leonard Pant's Ford Focus to the bus's rear hitch, secured our luggage and rolled out of the driveway. I turned on the radio, found some rock and roll and turned west, heading for Las Vegas. The plan was for me to drive the first day and after that we'd take turns. I settled into the driver's seat and prepared for a long day.

"Ah, Buck?" said Rusty. "It's right on the way...could we stop at the phone company so I can pay this bill? It's due and we won't be back until it's too late."

"It's on the way? Sure, okay." Rusty's idea of "on the way" involved a half-hour detour, but finally I got us turned west again.

Mink said, "Do you suppose we ought to get gas now, or wait?"

"Now's a good time, seeing as we only have an eighth of a tank."

We gassed up. We stopped at K-Mart for a road atlas. We stopped by Mink's sister's house to wake her up and borrow her camera. We went back to K-Mart for batteries. We waited in the Sooper-Dooper Burger parking lot while Rusty and Louis went in to buy us all breakfast sandwiches and coffees. We stopped so Leonard Pant could use the bathroom in the gas station next to Sooper-Dooper

Burger. Then I got us to I-94 and took the ramp that pointed to Chicago and we were off.

The southern part of Michigan that I-94 goes through is flat. That's not to say the road itself is flat. Some sections have new blacktop but lots of stretches seemed to have been untouched since the sixties. Mink was sitting in the seat behind me as I drove.

"Corn?" he asked, tapping at the side window.

"Soybeans, most likely," I answered.

"I think it's a weed farm," said Louis. "This is where they grow all the weeds that you see on the sides of the roads. They grow them here and then the Transportation Department takes them and plants them along all the freeways."

"Really?" said Mink. He can be amazingly gullible sometimes.

"Sure, haven't you ever seen those guys in the orange jumpsuits walking along the shoulder of the freeway with big plastic bags? That's them. They walk along and when they see a place with nothing growing, they dig a hole with their little stick and jam in a weed."

"Why not grass?" said Mink, getting just a bit suspicious.

"Because grass don't grow. Weeds grow. If grass grew there, they wouldn't need a weed farm. At least they're green," said Louis.

"I guess."

I'd wait until I could get him alone to see if Mink was really buying all of that and then set him straight. Maybe.

We'd left Interstate 94 in Chicago about eight o'clock. It had been clear and bright when we left home, but the sky had turned into one, low, putty-colored cloud. It was getting dark fast as we headed west on Wisconsin Route One. The tar strips made a nice thumping sound, identical to the beat of the theme song from "Saturday Night Fever." The wavy road gave the bus a slow roll and that caused the stuffed orangutan hanging from the sun visor to bump my head every twenty seconds. I swatted it out of the way.

"Hey," called Louis from his lawn chair, "you be nice to your twin brother."

"Why'd you buy this thing, anyway?" I called back. "So you wouldn't miss your girlfriend?"

He chucked a beer bottle cap at me, but there wasn't much velocity behind it. We were all tired. "Mink," I said, "where's this sweet little camp ground you said was up here?"

Mink shuffled some papers for a minute and said, "It's the North Eileen Schwartz Memorial Campground and it's just past Scander. Where are we at now?"

"We just went through Minenokawok a few miles back."

Leonard Pant asked, "When did we go through a town?"

"Remember when you dropped that peanut butter cup and bent down to find it? When you sat back up we were through. Was that the last of them cups? I'm hungry."

"Maybe," said Rusty, "we better stop at a MacDonald's in Scander."

"Maybe," I said, "we better stop right now."

A Sheriff's car was right behind us with its roof lights flashing blue and red. As I eased us over onto the shoulder they went to blue and yellow and a pair of spotlights lit us up. The county must have spent a thousand dollars on those lights. I saw the officer get out of the car and wondered if he'd come up to the driver's side window of the bus or the folding passenger door. He didn't seem too sure either, but after a little hesitation he picked the window side.

I slid it open and he called up, "License and registration, please."

I was a little nervous; I'd seen movies of cops getting shot by drivers who seemed to be reaching for their papers and came out with a gun. I'd also heard of drivers getting shot by cops who'd seen those movies and were understandably worried.

I kept my hands high on the steering wheel and called down, "The registration's over the sun visor and my license is in my wallet." I got them both and handed them down. "Was I speeding or something?"

He said, "Wait here," and went back to his car.

"Leonard," I said, "if you threw that peanut butter cup wrapper out the window and I get a littering ticket out of this, you're paying."

"I didn't throw nothing. What did you do Buck? Speeding?"

"No. It's a forty-five speed limit here. I was going about forty." I didn't mention the fact that if I'd sped up I'd have had to find a different song to match the tar strips.

After waiting about fifteen minutes the officer came back. "You got a burned out head lamp, your license plate is obscured by excessive dust and or dirt and your left front tire looks to be close to the three thirty-seconds of an inch of tread that the law allows. I might let you slide on the plate dirt and the tire tread, but I'm going to have to write you up for that head lamp."

From the back of the inside of the bus there was a huge clatter and Mink yelled out, "Wait a minute!"

When I looked back to the officer, his hand was twitching near the top of his holster.

I called down, "That's just Mink. This is his bus."

Mink opened one of the rear windows and stuck his head out calling, "Sir, if you'll just give me a minute or two, I know we packed a spare headlamp in here somewhere. I think it's behind the rain ponchos." He ducked in and rattled around some more. Within a minute he was waving the lamp out the window.

The officer looked perplexed. "I still can't let you go off with defective equipment on your vehicle."

Leonard Pant crammed himself between me and the steering wheel, leaned out the window and said, "Officer, we were just heading into Scander and we were going to stop and eat anyway. If you'd give us an official escort so we'd be safe till we got to a parking lot, we could fix it right there."

"Well…" said the cop.

"If I remember right," Leonard went on, "section three-fifty-seven of the motor vehicle code almost requires you to help a stranded motorist. Or maybe that was section eight-twelve."

"Requires?"

"Well, yeah. We can't leave the bus here all night because it'd be a traffic hazard. And I don't think there's a lot of towing companies out this way that might handle a bus this size. So, unless we're all getting arrested and you're going to fit us all in your back seat, we're stranded and that's why Bobbie Jo's Law got passed in the first place.

You remember those folks in Arizona? The Officer left half of them in their broken car in the middle of nowhere and the one of them tried to walk out and got bit by a rattlesnake and died? That was Bobbie Jo."

"Ahhh…"

"How far to Scander?" asked Leonard.

"Five miles," said the cop.

"We'll turn on our flasher and follow you, officer."

Leonard pulled back and sat down. Very quietly he said, "Start the bus."

I hesitated.

"Start the freaking bus," he hissed. He whispered to Mink, "The flashers do work, don't they?" Mink nodded.

We followed the police cruiser to Scander at exactly forty-five miles per hour. Between the increased speed and the rhythm of the flashers, the tar-strip beat stopped being disco and started to be something like a cross between a conga and a polka. I still hadn't found a song to match the beat before we pulled into the parking lot of the Scander Family Diner.

Three feeble yellow lights on a pole were barely enough to cast our shadows on the gravel, much less work by. The cop sat in his car and watched as the five of us huddled around the front of the bus. After about ten minutes he called out, "Okay, if you boys can get that fixed, I guess we don't have to worry about that ticket. Clean off the license plate. I see you again, it better be shiny." He wheeled out of the parking lot on his way to more adventures in defective equipment enforcement.

Changing a headlight should be easy. It's not. There are little screws and springs and adjusters. As soon as one of us started cussing, another would push him out of the way and start screwing and adjusting. It took about half an hour to change that light bulb.

Looking down the dark main street of Scander after we finished, Louis said, "No MacDonald's."

"No nothing," said Leonard Pant.

He was right. Night was full and there was no moon. There were no street lamps, no lights in the half-dozen shop windows and there wasn't even a bar in sight…just the steady blinking of the yellow traffic signal at the town's one intersection.

"Well," said Mink, "it's either the Scander Family Diner or we wait until we find the camp site, park the bus, set up camp and cook something ourselves."

Louis said, "I want breakfast. We can ask them in there where the campground is."

"Yeah," said Mink, patting his gut, "I haven't had a cheeseburger all day. My cholesterol is down about a quart."

We walked in. The linoleum was mostly a brown-flecked cream color that graded to gray around the bases of the chrome swivel stools at the counter. We slid into a corner booth. Three older women were sitting at the counter.

"Yow!" yelled Rusty as he tried to stand halfway back up. The women looked our way. The duct tape on the seat had lost its grip on some of the red vinyl upholstery and a ragged edge had grabbed at his butt. "Just like the Beer Bar," he muttered as he sat back down a little farther to the left.

I heard a squeak, squeak squeak. Rusty said, "Holy shit." I looked up to see our waitperson, Lois, walking toward us, her neon-trimmed sneakers chirping on the linoleum with every step. She was jammed into a pink, polyester waitress dress that a woman might have called two sizes too small. To a man it was two sizes just right, except that somehow all of that tightness had formed her breasts into a pair of nearly conical shapes, like she was wearing one of those pointy nineteen-fifties, rocket ship nose cone brassieres.

"Coffee?" she asked, pot in one hand and a hip in the other.

We jabbered orders of coffee and de-caf. She squeaked away. We watched. In his best, bad, Bogart impression Rusty said, "Of all the gin joints in all the world…."

"You like that stuff, Rusty?" said Mink.

Louis laughed, "She fits his idea of the perfect date…she's a mammal."

"Hey, she looks hot," said Rusty, "a few miles on her, maybe. But hot."

"Geez, you guys are something," I said. "She's just who she is and she looks how she looks. It takes more than tits to make a woman."

They probably were getting ready to say something back to me, but just then Lois squeaked back to take our orders. The guys were strangely polite. We ordered and when Lois brought our food Rusty asked if she knew where the North Eileen Schwartz Memorial Campground was.

She wrote directions on the back of the last clean napkin on the table and said, "That's how to get there, but I don't think it's open. There was a problem there this spring with some kids from New York and e. coli in the water." She got a call from the counter for a refill on the women's coffees. We started discussing our options. Luckily for us, our pal, Lois, had been busily solving our problem with the help of her three buddies at the counter. She came back to our booth, topped off our coffees and put down the pot.

"The way we see it," she said, motioning with her head to the trio at the counter, "you've got three options. Number one, maybe you're lucky and the Campground is open and the situation with the water is fixed. Number two, you could probably give Mr. Hansen at the Sunoco station ten dollars and he'd let you park behind his building. But he's got these two Rotweilers, so you probably wouldn't want to go for a little stroll in the middle of the night."

"I don't like dogs much," said Mink.

"Number three, the girls over there think you should just leave the bus here and go home with them. Personally, I think you'd be better off with Hansen's dogs, but I told the ladies I'd make the offer." With that a beeper went off near the cash register, meaning that either Lois had a phone call or the fries were done. Whichever it was, she went to check.

Rusty tipped his baseball cap at the ladies, the youngest of which was about sixty-three. He smiled and said, "Thanks, but no thanks." The one on the far right slapped the counter and laughed, saying, "Lois, honey, I can't believe you told him!"

Louis said, "Rusty, I think you're missing out on a good thing. Shoot, you're never in your life going to have another chance for a foursome."

"No," said Rusty, "but I'd sure settle for a twosome with little Miss Lois over there."

We finished eating and I paid the bill as the guys left. I followed them out to the bus. Climbing into the bus I had a sudden thought, "Hey, did we leave a tip?" We hadn't. I said, "I'll go back and take care of it and you guys can pay me back later."

Lois was cleaning up our mess as I walked up. "I'm sorry. We forgot to leave this."

"Thanks," she said, stuffing the bills in her pocket. "The other guys I wasn't so sure about, but I didn't think you'd stiff me on the tip."

"Aw, they're okay," I said.

"Yeah, right. What was that crack he made about this being a gin joint?"

"You heard?"

"Yup. The acoustics in here are funny. You can practically hear a person breathe in that booth from all the way over by the cash register. So I also know I got a few miles on me but that your one friend at least recognizes me as a mammal."

"I'm sorry…" I started.

"No. It's okay. I have to remember…how did that go, what you said? It takes more than tits to make a woman? Was that it?"

"Yeah."

She looked down at her chest. "Lost them both. Cancer. Eight years ago. I liked what you said."

I said goodnight and started walking toward the door, but she stopped me in front of the window. She asked, "Want to mess with your friend's heads?"

I must have grinned. She said, "Tell them this is my last night here. Tell them I'm moving to Texas in the morning. Tell them I'm sorry you have to go." Then she reached up and put her arms around my neck and gave me one, long, slow kiss. Then she backed off and smiled. "I wanted that to last long enough so I'd be sure that redheaded jerk who's with you would see. Good night. And by the way, you kiss good."

I floated back to the bus.

The guys went nuts. All except Rusty. He was real quiet. I just told them what she wanted me to say. I even polished it up a little. You never know how a kindness might come back to you.

I followed the napkin map toward the Campground.

"Here, Mink, you read this. I'm too busy driving."

Mink scrambled forward and took the official green lawn chair-navigator's position. "We're on County Road Twenty?"

"Yup," I said, although I was less than one hundred percent positive. The headlight we'd fixed back at the diner was bright as hell, but we'd pointed it down too far and all it lit up was a three-foot wide oval, four yards in front of us. One of those spring adjusters must have snapped. The other headlamp must have had a pretty thick layer of bugs and dirt on it because it scarcely shed any light at all. I was making about twenty miles per hour because I didn't want to miss a turn and have to back up a sixty-foot bus towing a car.

Mink said, "I'm guessing we make a right turn in about a mile. It sure is dark out here. I think the last light I saw was back at that diner. There's not even any cars out."

He was right. I couldn't remember seeing a single car either coming toward us or passing. And the blacktop was getting really rutty and might not even be blacktop any more…maybe just hard packed dirt.

"Slow down, Buck. Yeah, up there is a road off to the right. And, hey! Did you see that?"

"What?"

"We just passed a sign. It said, 'Blue Lake Township Camping Grounds,' and there was an arrow showing to turn right."

"I thought we were going to the North Eileen Schwartz Memorial Campground. What happened to that?" I asked.

"That girl back at the dinner said it might be closed. She must have just sent us to one she knew was open."

I turned right and we creaked up the road until it became a trail. There were mounds so close to the trail the weeds skreeked along both sides of the bus. "I don't see any campsites," I said.

"They're probably up closer to the lake."

"What lake?"

"Blue Lake...like it said on the sign. They are probably full up by the lake. If we park back here at the first spot you find, we might not even have to pay. There...take that first turn off. We can park there for the night and not disturb anybody."

I parked and killed the lights. I counted three distinct sets of snores.

"You want a beer before you go to sleep?" asked Mink.

"No. Thanks. I've been driving most of the day. I'm ready to crash right now." And that's what I did. I heard Mink rustle around for a few minutes and then his cot creaked and there were four distinct sets of snores. Mine made five.

Just before I woke up in the morning I was having a dream. In that dream the five of us had been camping at the Blue Lake Township Campground for a month. We'd fished every day and then just laid back in the warm sunshine and listened to the birds. There were lots of birds in that dream. Seagulls. Lots of them. And lots of fish, too. We'd caught so many fish the place was starting to smell like fish. In fact, it was becoming quite pungent.

"Sweet Jesus!" screamed Louis, and I jumped from my dream. We were all awake and staring out the windows. My dream had been pretty close to reality. Seagulls. Lots of them. They were yelling and wheeling in the sky and sitting on the roof and crapping on the hood. The fish smell part was pretty real too, considering the piles of garbage and trash surrounding us on three sides.

"Bucky, get us out of here," Louis hollered.

I'm not so good before my first cup of coffee and my first cigarette. It didn't look like coffee was going to happen any time soon, but at least I could smoke. I lit one and swung over to the driver's seat, still stiff from seven hours on thin foam.

"How can you smoke now?"

"Smells better than dead fish and bird shit, don't it? I've got to think."

Right and left of the bus were mounds of old trash with thick weedy bushes growing out of them. In front of us the trail descended into a deep, wide valley of garbage. Torn plastic trash bags flapped, cubes of bundled newspapers cascaded like a waterfall down the right side of the crater and a pair of refrigerators, one avocado in color and the other burnt orange stood at the crest of junk directly across from us about a hundred yards ahead. Seagulls were everywhere. I was thinking how I've always liked seagulls; how they can float in the air waiting for you to toss them a french-fry. I like how smooth they are and their clear, mean, yellow eyes. Even the way they…

"Buck!"

"Oh." I really needed that coffee. "Looks like the only way out is the way we came in. We have to back out."

"Well, okay then, back out," said Leonard Pant.

"Leonard, the trail is maybe seven feet wide and the bus is six feet wide and we have the Focus hooked on the back. I can't back us up two hundred yards hitched like that. Somebody's got to go back, unhitch the car and back it out before I can move the bus."

"Aw, shit," said Leonard, and he moved up to the door, "okay, let me out."

I opened the door, Leonard stepped out and four million flies came in. He made his way back to the car, flipped the hitch and backed down the trail. I started the bus and followed. It took about a half an hour to get us all backed up and rehitched. Then we spent another half-hour squirting Raid and swatting flies. We got the vast majority of them out, leaving only a hundred thousand or so in the bus. I squashed about half of those with the orangutan and threw him out.

"It was that babe in the diner. She was the one who gave us the directions," said Rusty.

"Yeah, but we saw the sign…'Blue Lake Township Camping Grounds.' Look, we're going to pass it in a minute. Slow down, Buck, there it is."

I slowed and as we passed the sign we read it, plain as could be, 'Blue Lake Township Dumping Grounds.'

"So, last night," said Louis, his voice a little shaky, "when I woke up and stepped outside to take a leak…that probably wasn't a raccoon

I pissed on, huh?"

"Tonight," said Mink, "we're sleeping in a motel."

I'd done most of the driving for the last thousand miles but in all that time I hadn't found a comfortable position to sit in. I supposed the designers of nineteen-eighty-one Blue Bird school busses hadn't spent much time considering ergonomics. With sixty eighth graders behind you and a stop every few minutes your mind wouldn't spend a lot of time considering your butt. It also didn't help that since we left the Blue Lake Township Dumping Grounds the stuffed orangutan had gotten caught in the seat adjuster mechanism and allowed only about three inches of fore and aft travel. I guessed he'd bounced off the window frame when I tried to dispose of him before. With the seat jammed Rusty and I were the only ones tall enough to reach the pedals, and there was some question as to whether or not he had a valid license. Mink was way too short and so was Leonard Pant. Louis is only about an inch shorter than me at six feet but he's put together funny. He's got short legs and short arms and I don't know how he can still look me level in the eye, but he can. I think it's like he's a giant dwarf.

Then "Do You Love Me" came on the radio and we sang that. Half way through "The Lion Sleeps Tonight" Rusty yelled that we sounded like shit so we shut up. I saw a sign and announced to no one in particular, "Davenport, Iowa, fifty-eight miles."

"You know what your trouble is?" asked Rusty.

I didn't know I had a trouble. "What?"

"You keep thinking about things like there was some complicated answer to everything. It's simple. Like what Freud said."

"Like what?"

"Sex. That's what's behind everything."

"Everything?"

"Sure. He said every time you see a flat thing you think of bed and when you think of bed, you think of sex. And every time you see a tubular thing you think of your penis. And everything with a hole in it makes you think of a woman's vagina. Simple."

"Hmmm," said Louis pointing out the bus window. "So, when

you see that, what are you supposed to think about?" They were putting in big drainage pipes along the road. One after another were these big concrete pipes, probably each five feet high and forty feet long.

"Is that a long tubular thing or a hole?"

"It's a long tubular thing, you jerk. Can't you see? Long and round and if Freud saw it he'd say it was just a perfect penis reminder."

"Yeah, but it's got a hole. It's practically nothing but hole. Isn't that supposed to represent a woman's vagina? I mean you're the Freud guy here, what do you say Doctor Wise Ass?"

"I say it's a penis and that's what it is."

"I guess," I said, "it kind of depends what you're looking for. Seems to me that Louis has got vaginas on the brain. And you got penises."

"Hey. What are you trying to say?" Rusty was getting a little pissed.

"I'm not saying anything. You're the one who told us all about this sex thing."

Louis said, "So, this guy goes to a psychiatrist…"

"Yeah?" I said, sensing a joke coming on.

"And the psychiatrist says, 'Here, I want you to look at these pictures.' And he holds up this ink-blot and says, 'What do you see?'

"The guys says, 'Whoa, that there's a picture of a man and a woman and they're having sex.'

"So the psychiatrist says, 'Okay, how about this one,' and he holds up another one.

"And the guys says, 'Geez, that's a picture of a guy and three women and they're all having wild sex in the middle of the shopping mall.'

"The psychiatrist says, 'What do you see in this one?' and the guy says, 'Yow, that's four guys and eleven women and they're doing every kind of sex thing you can think of to each other.'

"'Well,' says the doctor, 'I can see that you're nothing but a sex maniac with nothing but sex on your mind.'

"And the guy says, 'Hey, Doc, not me, you're the one with all the dirty pictures.'"

Rusty laughed and went back to his seat to continue his breast patrol.

The radio news guy told us that the population of the earth was now something like six point two billion, and without missing a beat Louis said, "If you took everybody on earth and squashed them into a box, how big a box would it be?"

"Louis," I said, "this is getting too weird."

We crossed the Mississippi looking into the remains of a salmon pink sunset and pulled off the freeway at the first exit we came to.

"A Holiday Inn or a Ramada," said Mink. "There's both of them in this town."

"I don't care," said Rusty, "as long as it's not a campground in Scander."

"Cheap," said Leonard Pant. "It's got to be cheap. Remember, we had planned on camping all the way out to Vegas and back. We go staying at high priced places, we won't have anything left when we get there."

"That sounds right to me," I said. "I'd rather save my money for the blackjack tables, but I'd rather not have to find a campground tonight. Let's get a burger someplace and check out the yellow pages."

I drove through town, the town being Martin, Nebraska, looking for a fast food place. Up ahead was a red, blinking neon sign saying, "Hamburgers." We stopped, got our burgers and sat at a window booth.

"These are good," said Mink, wiping his chin. "This place isn't part of a chain, I bet. Tastes homemade."

We borrowed a phone book and found a listing for a local motel on a main road, just outside of town. We took two rooms and I got a nap in a real bed. That night the five of us sat in one of the rooms eating take-out fried chicken.

"I needed that nap," I said. "What did you guys do?"

"I got a little nap, too," said Mink.

"We went exploring," said Rusty.

"Yeah, we explored," said Leonard Pant. "This guy," he nodded toward Rusty, "has a nose for sleaze."

"Thanks," said Rusty.

"He gave me directions like he'd lived in this town his whole life. Right to the only X-rated movie house within a hundred miles, and he says, 'turn right, turn left, go straight,' and sure as heck there's the Kitty-Kat Theater."

"It's a gift," said Rusty. "And don't tell me you didn't like it."

"I've seen X-rated movies before, Rusty," said Louis. "There were some odd guys standing around the door though."

"Didn't notice," said Rusty.

We practiced playing blackjack for a while and looked at a couple of maps of Las Vegas that Mink had printed up on his computer.

"A couple more days driving, Buck?" asked Rusty.

"Yeah," I said, "with decent traffic and weather, I think two more full days. Mink, you do, for sure, have directions to the campground we're going to in Vegas."

"Yup."

"And reservations?"

"Yup," and he patted his pocket.

It was getting near midnight and my nap was wearing off. Louis and Mink agreed, so the three of us took one room. Rusty and Leonard Pant went to the other room to deal some more blackjack and practice shooting craps. I drifted off to sleep wondering how a person could practice rolling sevens.

We got up early the next day and finished off Nebraska before noon. I didn't want to trust the bus at high altitudes, so when we got to the Rockies, I turned left. Louis used a pillow and drove for a few hours so I got to see the world from a side window instead of the windshield. It was the same world, but my right leg appreciated the rest.

Near the Colorado, New Mexico border we found a camp ground right where the guidebook said it would be. We set up for the night. It was hot.

"Mink, let's unscrew the stove from the floor and bring it outside," I said. "It's plenty hot in here without cooking dinner." We tried to get the Coleman loose, but we'd done too good a job of screwing in into the floor.

"There's a camp store up where we checked in," said Louis. "I think I saw firewood." He walked up to the store with Leonard Pant and they came back with two armloads of wood. Leonard grumbled about the price.

We arranged about half of the wood in a small pit. Actually Rusty did the arranging, claiming he had vast experience in that area. After twenty minutes, the folks in the site next to ours took pity and lent us a squirt of lighter fluid.

While I opened a few big cans of hash and a giant tin of green beans, Leonard Pant took the grill off the Coleman stove and put it over the fire. Rusty got nominated to be hash stirrer and we each opened a beer. For the next three hours we stared at the fire and burped hash and talked. It got to be the kind of talk that only happens when there's no TV and you're with friends and you're gathered around a fire with a beer in your hand. I learned that Mink had been married before which was a shock because it seemed that Mink and Mrs. Mink had been together since the beginning of time. I learned that Rusty had been held back in second grade. That wasn't so much of a shock. Leonard Pant talked about the hardware business. I told them the story about Uncle Vern and the portable toilet. After that my eyeballs were starting to feel all sandy from staring at the fire and I started yawning. We all went to bed.

We were up early the next morning. With luck we'd hit Vegas by nightfall, and luck was with us. With only gas stops and a lunch break we made good time. Even a couple of stops at souvenir stands didn't slow us down too much, although the argument Leonard Pant got into with the fellow selling turquoise, pretty much assured that we'd have to take a different route home. If it hadn't been for that we would have left Arizona in daylight. As it was, we didn't cross the Nevada state line until after nine o'clock.

Still miles away from Vegas, we could see a hot bright glow in the sky. We crested a hill, and there below us in the valley was the city. Everybody stared out the right side windows at the quiet, brilliant swarm of light.

"Are we going through town?" asked Leonard Pant.

Mink consulted his travel guide. "No. We turn off before we get to town. The campground is west a few miles."

"How about later? After we set up?"

My butt was tired. I said, "Tomorrow will be soon enough for me. By the time we get set up it'll be after midnight."

"Vegas never sleeps," said Rusty.

"I do," I answered. "If any of you guys want to take the Focus into town, that's up to you."

I followed Mink's directions and found Meadowlands Park with no problem.

"Sounds like the name of a cemetery," said Leonard Pant. I didn't answer.

We registered at the park store and followed Marigold Circuit to Dew Petal Lane. It was a good thing we had reservations. The place was quite full. We pulled in, unhooked the Focus and I jiggled the bus back and forth until we were level enough for our beer bottles not to slide off the table. It was nearly midnight, but, as Rusty said, Vegas never sleeps. Neither did the campground. There was music on all sides of us and a little shouting, but as tired as I was, I didn't think it would bother me.

We swung the bunks down and got our stuff settled. Rusty and Leonard Pant were going to do a quick tour of the city before bed. They'd had some sleep while I had driven.

"We'll see you guys later," called Rusty. Leonard got behind the wheel of the little Ford.

"Buck," he called, "toss me the key."

"I don't have the key," I said. "Last one to have the key was you, when you backed out when we were in the dump in Scander."

"I gave them back to you."

"Nope," I said. "I was busy driving the bus. I didn't take any keys from you. Rusty, it's your car. Do you have a spare set on you, or hidden or something?"

"Sure, I got a spare set of keys," said Rusty. "Right on my dresser at home. I thought they'd be safe there if we lost the ones we had."

I decided not to try to work my way through the logic of that thought process.

"So what are we going to do?" asked Leonard.

I said, "I guess we just unhitch the Focus and drive the bus when we want to go into town. And that's not going to be tonight. Maybe tomorrow we can find a Ford dealer and see if they can make us some new keys."

After a bit of expected grumbling we began to settle in to our campsite. We had some canned spaghetti for dinner and sat around playing poker. The night was warm and there was a lot of music in the air; Latin salsa from our east and Elvis songs from our west. We heard lots of talking; Spanish to the east and Anglo to the west. There was the low growling of a dozen generators at the neighboring campsites. It was just plain loud. The closer to midnight it got, the louder it got. A short while later a fight broke out on our western border. I walked over to see what was going on.

It didn't turn out to be much of a fight; just some pushing and shoving between two guys. They were surrounded by thirty or forty other guys who were mostly shouting and shaking fists at one another. I didn't see any weapons although one fellow was holding another at bay with a can of Silly String.

I asked a guy standing off to the side what was going on.

"Noise," he said.

"Yeah, plenty of that," I said.

"These folks over there," he motioned to the east, "we're here for our family reunion. See?" He pointed past our bus to a bright yellow banner flapping over a huge fifth-wheel camping trailer. It read, "Rodriguez Family Reunion." Other yellow banners read, "Chavez," and "Melina," and "Cardoza."

"I'm a Rodriguez, myself," he said. "This is our first night here. I thought we had the whole campground reserved, but I guess not. We only have about half of it. They have the rest." He pointed west.

"They? Another family?"

"Kind of. They sure look alike, don't they?"

I had to admit that they was more than a passing resemblance among the folks to the west. They all shared the same color of coal black hair. And sideburns—even the women. And sequins—even the men. Especially the men.

"They're here for an Elvis impersonator convention," he said.

I figured that would explain the large number of jumpsuits.

"So, okay," I said, "Rodriguez over here and Elvises over there. Why is this a problem?" The two guys fighting were now on the ground. I still hadn't seen any punches thrown, but the Elvis had three colors of Silly String hanging from his left sideburn.

"Noise, like I said. Last night it was "Blue Suede Shoes" until four-thirty in the morning, and it was loud. Tonight some of the younger members of the Cardoza family showed up with reinforcements."

"More family members?" I asked.

"More speakers," he answered. At least I'm pretty sure that's what he answered. Just at that moment the air filled with a massive thumpa-thumpa-thumpa beat. I could hear it in my liver. I looked and saw a pickup truck in the Cardoza camp. In the bed were six speakers, each the size of a four drawer filing cabinet. A teenage Cardoza was standing on the speakers and yelling something at the Elvises. I think he was yelling. Who could tell?

"Why?" I screamed in my new friend's ear, "why?"

"They started it," he yelled back. He pointed to a number of posts standing up amongst the Elvises. On top of each post were four speaker horns. "They put them up last night. We couldn't hear our own music. We couldn't hear anything. One of the New Mexico families found an ax and chopped their power cord. They got kind of mad, they fixed the cord and then really cranked up the volume." Over the shuddering thumpa-thumpa-thumpa he said, "But I think we've got them tonight."

"Maybe not," I answered.

Two flat bed trucks pulled into the Elvis compound. Both carried at least a half dozen black boxes, each the size of an industrial strength refrigerator. They weren't refrigerators. They were speakers. I headed back to the bus.

We pulled the cotton out of a Tylenol bottle and made enough earplugs for everybody except Mink and me. He found an old pair of earmuffs at the bottom of the storage cabinet. I got the earphones and Rusty's CDplayer. The earphones didn't stop much of the noise so I played the only CD he had brought. By six in the morning I had heard all the Gordon Lightfoot I would ever need for the rest of my life. Actually, long before the trip I had heard all of the Gordon Lightfoot I would ever need. This was just a bonus.

In the semi-calm of morning we packed our things, checked out of the campground headed into Vegas to find a hotel.

Traffic was awful. Every vacant lot had something being built on it and it seemed that half of the places that were already built were being torn down to put up something new. There were also not nearly enough lanes on the roads to handle the traffic. To fix this problem they decided to close half of the lanes they did have to resurface them. There were orange cones everywhere. It took five minutes to make a right turn onto The Strip. It didn't help that we were in a full sized bus with a keyless Ford hitched to our bumper.

"There," said Leonard Pant, "Ming's Palace...turn in there."

"I can't, Leonard, it's too sharp of a turn. We'll smash one of those concrete statues."

Several minutes and about a hundred yards later he said, "What about there? The Fiji Hotel. We could use their parking lot and walk around to find a place to stay."

The driveway was wide enough so I put on my turn signal and nudged the nose of the bus to the right. The problem was that the constant stream of people on the sidewalk never stopped. It was like forty feet of bright yellow school bus was invisible to them. After a long time Rusty got out to hold up the pedestrians until I could get in. He'd get one batch of them stopped but then some stragglers would get through and the batch would follow them. We needed our own orange cones. I gave up and waved Rusty back to the bus.

"We'll get off the Strip at the next light, I'll find us a grocery store or someplace to park and we'll walk back or take a cab or something." It took nearly an hour, but I got us to a little factory about three blocks off the strip and put the bus in the rear of their parking lot. A guy driving a hi-lo gave us a funny look but didn't say anything. We walked to the strip, and back to the Fiji.

A tour group of about a hundred people were standing in the check in area so I found an Information sign and waited for a clerk. The long and short of it was that this was a very full week for conventions in Las Vegas and although they had some rooms, they were going at full price, well over two hundred dollars a night.

"Two hundred dollars?" said Leonard Pant. "That's a good chunk of what a package tour would have cost."

"I guess they're pretty full," I answered. "We can check around."

After phoning a few hotels we found that it was full everywhere. There was no way our budget could afford that kind of money. We sat at a bar in Ming's Palace to think about things.

"Okay, look," said Louis, "we don't have to be staying at some big hotel. We'll make some calls and find a nice little place off the Strip. A motel, not a hotel. It's not like we'll be spending much time in the rooms anyway, we'll be out doing things all the time."

Louis was right; we would have been staying in the bus anyway, so we sent Leonard and Rusty to find a cheap place to sleep and the three of us started to explore the casino. We all agreed to meet in an hour at the bar.

Louis and Mink and I scouted around the main floor, dropping occasional quarters into promising looking slot machines. Mink hit one for a buck. A long, fancy escalator went to the upper floors where the sports book and convention halls and more slots were. Louis plunked a quarter into the slot nearest the top of the elevator and hit for ten dollars. Mink sat at the one next to him but I decided to walk around a bit.

Around a corner I found a long, wide hall with some tables lined up along the side and a bunch of people milling around. A cardboard sign on a tripod pointed to the registration desk for the, "North American and Southwest Canadian Alternative Lifestyles Gathering." A fellow dressed all in black with a hint of glitter on his eyelids handed me a welcome folder.

"Hi! I'm Mar," he said. I looked at his clothes. He looked at my clothes. "You're here with the Midwesterners, I'd say." Michigan is in the Midwest. "Yeah," I answered, "we're from Michigan."

"Michigan!" he exclaimed, like he'd lived there all his life and thought I might know his aunt. "Never been there," he said, "but I owned a Buick once." That must have been a joke, because he laughed. "And who is the "we" you're talking about?"

"Well, there's me and four other guys. They're around here somewhere playing the slots."

"Oh, aren't they just everywhere?" said Mar. "And five of you! I never had much luck with odd numbers. Are you boys registered yet?"

"Nope. We're just exploring."

"Aren't we all?" said Mar. "Oh, look! It's Robert and Lori!" A very nice looking couple was walking toward us, hand in hand. "That Robert, he's such a boy."

"Huh?"

"Honestly, I'm as tolerant as the next person, but he's just so queer."

"Oh," I said. I was beginning to guess that Alternative Lifestyles didn't have anything to do with folks who preferred solar heating or lived underground.

"But it's fine," said Mar, tugging at the pleats of his slacks. "And he certainly loves to talk about it. You'll see."

"Robert! Lori! So nice to see you here." They exchanged hellos and hugs and kisses. "Here, you two. This is my new friend…ah…"

"Buck."

"Buck. Of course. Buck. You're Buck from Michigan, aren't you, darling? And dear Buck is so late, too. You haven't even registered yet, have you?"

"Michigan," I said. "Registered? Ah, well, no…"

He spotted another guy dressed in all black. "Must run…kisses everyone," called Mar as he scooted away.

"You're not really here for the convention, are you?" said Robert.

"Not really. I think Mar kind of assumed things. The convention…it's for…?"

"Alternative lifestyles. We all live in ways that don't involve you're typical Mom, Dad and two-point-one kids. Like Mar. He and his spouses are into a group, gay marriage thing. Lots of CDs here, too. Cross dressers. Like them," and he nodded to a pair of very pretty women. "And there are the poly-amorists and the celibate fetishists. Also a certain number of inter-racial couples."

"Inter-racial, is that Alternative?"

Robert said, "It is when you're like those two." He nodded to a small-eyed white girl holding hands with a Klingon.

"And you," I said feeling all brave and liberal, "you're gay, huh?"

Robert chuckled, "No, hardly that."

"But Mar just said…I mean, I thought…"

"No, please, don't be embarrassed. You couldn't have known, and that Mar is such a scamp sometimes. Here's the thing. I'm a woman." Robert scratched at his perfect beard.

"Oh."

"Yes, indeed," said Robert, "I'm a woman…trapped in the body of a man. I've known it for years. Fifteen, at least. From just before we got married." He put his arm around Lori's shoulder.

"Trapped?"

"Sure. Some accident of birth or brain chemicals or something, but I know what I am and what I am is a woman."

I looked back and forth between the two of them, "So…but…you and her…you're married? And Lori? You're a woman? Or…?"

"Yes," said Lori, "I'm all woman."

"So…?" I started.

"Well, Buck, the woman I am on the inside?" said Robert.

"Yeah?"

"She's a Lesbian."

I stammered something.

"Fortunately for me," Robert went on, giving Lori a little hug, "so is my wife." I blinked. "But now we really must get going. So nice meeting you."

They turned and walked away. I looked at the backs of their tee shirts. Each shirt had an arrow pointing toward the other person and in block print each shirt read, "I'm with her." I went to find Louis and Mink. Then the three of us rounded up Rusty and Leonard Pant.

They had gotten us reservations at the Sun Shade Motel. We reclaimed the bus from the factory parking lot, drove to the motel and checked in. Louis, Mink and I took one room and Rusty and Leonard got the other, which was right next door. We were settled in by two in the afternoon and spent a few minutes around a tiny table in Rusty's room looking at a street map of Vegas.

"This isn't so bad," said Leonard. "It looks like we're right between the Strip and Downtown. If it weren't a hundred and ninety degrees outside we could walk places."

"We can split cab fare," I said. "There are cabs everywhere, and busses too."

"We've got a bus," said Rusty.

"I mean a bus that I don't have to drive."

"Right. So, what do you say? Let's go downtown and see what's up."

We followed our map and found a bus that dropped us right at Fremont Street, downtown. We might have done a little more exploring but Leonard turned us into the first casino we came to. "We'll play a couple of hours and then see what we want to do," he said.

I know how to play Black Jack. You don't just bet your money and hope for the best. There are real guidelines and formulas you can follow to make your odds of winning better, and I usually remember enough to play smart about eighty-five percent of the time. I do that and hope I play right and then I hope for the best. After an hour, I was ahead nearly a hundred dollars. Then I got bored and took a break at a quarter slot machine.

From where I sat I could see the other guys. Leonard and Rusty were playing Black Jack a few tables down from where I had been. Leonard was intent, his eyes didn't move much and neither did the rest of him. He sat like a hunter in a blind. With every deal he'd make the proper little hand gestures to let the dealer know what he wanted. He rarely said anything, but Rusty said enough for the two of them. Rusty also waved his arms and talked too loud and pretended he knew what he was doing. He hit when he should have stayed and he doubled down at crazy times, but as odd as his betting was, he still won. He also made it a practice to make off the wall comments to the cocktail waitresses.

Mink played a few dollars on the Wheel of Fortune and then moved over to slot machines. The whole time he played he had a funny, concerned look on his face like he expected someone to come over and quiz him on what the odds were for three red sevens to come up. He lost steadily. Louis couldn't stay still. He played Black Jack at my table for ten minutes, then wandered around for another ten before sitting in at another table for three hands. Then he went to the slots and bounced from machine to machine like he was looking for one that fit.

I saw other people playing slots who didn't even bother to watch what came up with each spin. They'd just push the "Max Bet" button and listen for the electronic thunk, thunk, thunk, and then push it again, the whole time gazing around the casino or staring off into space. Other folks carried on running conversations while absently pushing the button. People swear they love to play the slots, but I don't know if I've ever seen any who actually looked like they were having fun.

Leonard and Rusty were ready to take on another casino, but I'd had more than enough for a while. So had Mink and Louis. "Okay," I said, "how about we split up for a while and meet back here in about two hours? Then we can decide about dinner."

"Oh yeah," said Rusty, "dinner. A buffet. One of them that's got all you can eat prime rib and shrimp and everything. One of those."

That sounded good to all of us. Rusty and Leonard headed up Fremont Street in search of a lucky table. Mink and Louis went into the first tee shirt shop they saw. I bought a bottled orange juice from a little store just off Fremont. Then I found a bench in the shade where I could sip my drink and watch people pass by.

I saw a crowd of about a dozen Japanese tourists stop in front of a casino doorway. One at a time and then in couples they stood at the entry while one of their party took their pictures. Twelve people, twelve pictures. Then they moved down to a poster advertising the casino's evening show, "The Bobby Roberts Spectacular." Twelve people, twelve more pictures. I lost interest when they started posing beside a drinking fountain.

I saw newlyweds and old people and groups of middle-aged women in colorful shorts and men in equally colorful shorts as well as some wearing expensive suits and sunglasses and using cell phones. I saw cops on bicycles and a clown with a head three feet in diameter and lots of families with little kids. I saw a woman with a three-year-old in tow, walking toward the benches where I sat. She was very drunk. She reeled and swayed and then leaned against a newspaper box for a minute before shoving off and staggering another twenty feet.

I'm not a do-gooder. If I see somebody doing something stupid to themselves, I generally let them go ahead and be stupid. But generally doesn't include times when the stupid person is in charge of a toddler. I stood up and walked toward the stumbling mom. I was making up lots of irate things to say, but when I got within three feet of her, she lurched and fell towards me. I caught her in my arms but that caught me off balance and we both went down to the pavement.

I sat with my butt on the concrete and her sitting between my legs, her back supported by my left shoulder and arm. Her dark glasses had fallen aside and she had an open-eyed stare. I couldn't smell any alcohol on her breath.

"Are you okay?" I asked. She mumbled something that might have been her son's name because he came over to her.

"Is this your mum?" I asked the boy. He didn't answer. "She gets sick sometimes, huh?"

He nodded. The nod might have just meant that he'd seen her drunk before, but I didn't think so.

"What's your name?" I couldn't understand his answer because his thumb was in the way. He was starting to tear up. I said, "Okay, buddy, I'm going to get some help but I've got to yell real loud to do that. But don't be scared when I yell because it's a good yell. You listen and tell me if I yell good." He watched me very closely and I put on a big smile and yelled, "Medic!" as loud as I could. "Was that good?" I asked. He nodded. A young couple trotted up to us.

"What's wrong?"

"I don't know. Get somebody. Go in this casino and get somebody." A crowd was starting to form. The woman woke for a second, saw her son and went out again. I was afraid to let go of her or lay her down on the hot cement or anything. I just held her. She was thin and quite pretty. I realized that in holding her up, my left arm was under hers and my hand was just under her breast. In the ninety seconds it took for someone to finally dash out the casino door I had time to worry that she'd suddenly wake up, feel my hand on her body and scream. I also had time to notice that my arm was cramping. The twelve Japanese tourists were taking pictures.

The casino worker arrived and said, "Does this happen often? Does she have medicine?"

"I don't know. I was just here when she fell. Somebody keep track of her kid. Blue shorts and a white tee shirt." The crowd was getting thicker. Then I saw him standing next to the clown with the big head.

"I bet she's got sugar," said someone in the crowd. A restaurant packet of sugar appeared from an outstretched hand.

"But wait," I said. "There's two kinds of blood sugar things. One you give sugar to but the with other I don't think you do." There were lots of faces over us. She gave a little lurch with her left arm and that pulled her blouse over my left forearm and landed her tit in my hand. It was cool to the touch.

Two bike cops skidded up and cleared the crowd back. From somewhere a box of fruit punch appeared and one of the cops was holding it to her lips. She was able to sip a bit. "Your wife?" he asked. I explained. He looked at my hand. "She fell this way. We both fell down. I've been afraid to move since." He nodded and listened to his ear piece radio. "EMS will be here in a minute."

The white and red EMS truck pulled up, two techs got out and spoke to the cops. One of them asked, "Your wife?" I explained again.

They put her on a stretcher, loaded her and her son into the ambulance and rolled away. The crowd slowly broke up. I stood up and looked around. Except for the fruit punch soaking the front of my shirt it was like nothing had happened. I walked back to my bench and sat down.

Louis and Mink found me about five minutes later and just as they sat down Rusty and Leonard walked up. I told them what had happened. I showed them my fruit punch stain. I skipped the part about her tit in my hand.

"I never even got her name," I said. That made me sad. I wished I could call a hospital and find out how she was and how her kid was and everything. I didn't want a thank you. I just would have liked to have known.

"So," said Rusty, "did you cop a feel?"

Mink said, "Rusty, is that the only thing you can think to say?"

"Yeah. So did you? I mean you said you kind of had her in your arms, right? She was leaning on you? You got a handful. I know you did."

"Nope," I said. "It all happened pretty fast. Even if it had all happened pretty slow, I don't think I would have thought about doing that." That was true…I didn't think about doing it…it just happened. I almost told Rusty that I preferred my women to be conscious. In fact I not only want her to be conscious, I want her to be Tangee.

"And she was cute? Nice shape? And you never even got a little fondle in? Damn. So where did this happen?"

"Over there. In front of Mike Chancey's Casino."

Rusty asked, "Did anybody from the casino know what you were doing?"

"No. Yeah. One guy from the casino came out. I think he was the one who called the police."

"What was his name? Was he like some boss or supervisor or somebody?"

"I don't think so. His name was Jason. It was printed on his green vest." I had no idea how I remembered all of that. "And he was young and blonde and had a kind of weasel face. No beard or moustache.

Skinny kid." It was like looking at a picture I didn't know my mind had taken. I could see him plain as anything.

"This might not be a total loss, yet," said Rusty. "Come on."

Rusty led us into the casino lobby. The rush of cold air raised goose bumps on me.

"Could I see a manager, please," Rusty said at the desk.

"What's this about," I asked.

"Just shut up and go along. You'll see."

A young black guy wearing a navy blazer with the casino's logo embroidered on its breast pocket came up and asked how he could help.

"There was quite a little problem just outside your door a short while ago," said Rusty. "A problem with a lady who had fallen down?"

The manager looked nervous. So was I. Rusty wasn't going to try to scam something on a bogus slip and fall claim was he? "Yes. I heard about it," said the manager.

"Well, I just want to say that your young man, Jason, certainly made your place look good. Very professional, mister...?" The manager handed his card to Rusty. He was Mister Writtley. "Thank you," said Mister Writtley. "Yes, Jason. He's new here, but I understand he made the call. Unfortunate thing. I don't really know what happened, but we're always glad when our employees do well."

Rusty went on, "I think some sort of bonus for Jason would be the right thing to do."

"I'm sure Jason's supervisor has already been told and we'll be sure that he's properly taken care of."

"Speaking of that," said Rusty, "you might not have known, but this man right here, was the guy who stayed with that poor woman through the whole thing."

"Really?"

"Yup. And he's the one who shouted, 'Somebody run into Mike Chancey's Casino. They're good people in there. They'll help.'"

"He said that?"

"Yup."

"You said that?" he asked me.

"It all happened pretty fast. That might not have been exactly it, but yeah, I was the one who yelled."

The manager smiled at Rusty. "It's a good thing you mentioned all of this. Come with me."

I whispered, "If you're getting me in some kind of trouble…"

We got to Mister Writtley's office. "Are you fellows here with your wives? No? Just the five of you? Here. Compliments of Mike Chancey. Tickets to our spectacular show. It's dark tonight, but if you stop by tomorrow and show these and you'll have center seats in the front section."

"And free drinks?" asked Rusty.

Writtley reached back into his desk and came up with more tickets. "Free drinks. Just show the card."

We all thanked Mister Writtley and he thanked us as he showed us out.

"Not bad," said Leonard Pant.

"Easy," said Rusty. "Shoot, tell a casino manager one of his people sneezed funny and they'll comp you something. I would have hit him up for the dinner buffet, but I noticed a sign when we came in that said the buffet is closed for remodeling."

"That's okay," said Mink, "that's great. We get to see a show. A real Las Vegas show."

We hopped a cab back to our motel. The guys wanted to spend some time at the pool but I just wanted a shower and a nap. I put my fruit punch stained shirt in the bathtub and turned on the shower. I washed the stickiness off of me and stomped around on my shirt. Both of us came clean. Then I made sure the air was cranked on high and flopped on the bed. I had some odd dreams but when I woke up I couldn't remember them, except that the clown with the three-foot head was in there somewhere.

The guys came back from the pool after about an hour and a half. Louis and Leonard Pant were pink.

"There's girls here," said Mink. "Lot's of them."

"Kids," said Rusty. "Teen group of some kind from Arizona. They won a trip here for doing something at school."

"Some of them are older than kids," said Mink.

"Those ones are college freshmen," said Rusty. "They are kind of like the chaperones for the younger ones. A few of them might not be too bad looking if they fixed themselves up. I asked one of them. They said it's this church school and they've got all the grades from kindergarten through twelfth grade and right across the street is this two year junior college they all go to when they graduate."

I asked, "I wonder what church school sends their kids to Vegas for a fieldtrip?"

"Whatever," said Rusty. The girls were too young and not cute enough so he wasn't interested.

"Ready for dinner?" I asked.

"A buffet? Heck, yeah, I'm ready," said Mink. "Which one should we go to? There's a lot of them around."

Leonard Pant said, "Let's go to Ming's Palace. I saw a sign when we were there."

A quick cab ride took us to Ming's. We waited in the buffet line for about ten minutes and didn't seem to be moving.

"Let's go up ahead and scout out the buffet," said Rusty. "Mink, you wait here and hold our place."

We got far enough ahead to get a look at the food. "Damn," said Leonard Pant, "it looks like a school cafeteria line." It did look that way. The whole buffet, except for a separate desert table was only about twelve feet long, there wasn't much variety and what was there didn't look all that good.

I said, "All I can eat of that is nothing. Let's go." Mink objected, but then he hadn't seen the food. "I guess," I went on as we flagged another cab, "what we'd better do is ask somebody, like this cabby." A five-year-old Lincoln Town Car with a taxi light on its roof pulled over, its tires making a soft squeal on the hot pavement. We piled in and asked the driver what the best buffet in town was, and he said the one at the El Grecco Hotel. He took us there.

We walked through the casino following the signs for the Neptune Buffet. We went past the slot players and the life-size model of the Parthenon and a number of marble statues of naked men with small penises and naked women with small breasts. It looked like the men got the better of the deal. We finally came to another marble statue, this one of Neptune. Neptune was quite a lot bigger all the way around. He was guarding the entrance to his buffet. The line wasn't too long at all.

Mink was staring at Neptune. "Roman," he said. "Neptune was the Roman god of the sea. Poseidon was the Greek one."

"So?" said Leonard Pant.

"So, nothing. Just funny that a hundred million dollar Greek theme hotel would get that wrong."

I was surprised Louis didn't come up with that one, but he smiled when he heard Mink and made a little note in his book. The line moved up nicely and we were seated in fifteen minutes.

The main buffet table had to be close to seventy feet long and it curved is an S shape from one side of the room to the other. There were separate, oval tables for salad and bread and desert. Rusty was first up to the buffet line and back to the table before we'd even started. His plate had a big slab of prime rib on it but it was half buried in shrimp.

"That's all you got?" asked Mink. "They've got tons of other stuff up there. There's five different kinds of potatoes and vegetables and more kinds of salad fixings than I've ever seen."

"Potatoes," said Rusty around a mouthful of beef, "that's what they want you to eat so you don't get so much of the good stuff. Potatoes are twenty cents a pound, prime rib like this is twenty bucks. I'm not stupid." He was peeling shrimp as he chewed.

By the time the rest of us returned to the table with our first plates, Rusty was ready for his second. Mink had been to the salad bar and brought back two slices of tomato, a little mound of raw spinach and some black olives. He cut his tomatoes carefully and chewed slowly. Louis had one plate of various salads and another with chicken stir-fry. Leonard Pant just had prime rib and a baked potato. I had some of everything I could reach.

"I just like regular food," said Leonard. "Nothing fancy or things that I don't know what's in them. Meat and potatoes. The shrimp looks good too. I'll be back for some of those."

"Rusty," said Louis, "you're going to make yourself sick." Rusty wasn't listening. It was like he was on a mission to eat as many dollars worth of food as he could hold. That's not to say that the rest of us were exactly holding back. I wanted to try a taste of everything on those tables but I knew the odds were against me. The problem with wanting to try everything is that once you find something really good, you're too full to eat much of it.

Mink, taking his time, had worked his way through most of the seafood's before he pushed his plate back and said, "That's it for me. Wow, was that good."

"Hell," said Rusty, "I wouldn't even call that a good start." Rusty was slowing down. "I'll bet I ate thirty dollars worth of food so far," he said.

People get funny at buffets. Rusty wasn't funny, but he was looking kind of queasy. He told us he thought a plateful of those fancy deserts would settle him down, but we talked him out of it.

We had planned on taking a walking tour of the casino and the few blocks around it, but even at ten in the evening the temperature was over ninety. Besides that, Rusty was holding his stomach and walking pretty slowly so we decided to call it a night and head back to the motel. He objected, but not too much.

We hung around the pool for a while, drinking beer and enjoying the desert breeze. When Rusty saw there weren't any women at the pool he decided to go inside and digest his dinner for a while. In fact we all thought it was odd that none of the schoolgirls were at the pool that night. We chatted until past midnight, which is three in the morning Michigan time, and went to bed.

I'd had a hard time calling Tangee with the time zone difference and everything. She didn't exactly understand how it could be one time for her and another time for me. I think she thought it was just an excuse not to call her. But I did call every day and left messages most of the time. I was down to one bar on my phone battery and had left my charger at home.

Friday morning Rusty was wondering if we could find an all you could eat breakfast buffet. We told him no.

"Okay," I said as we finished our bacon and eggs at the motel coffee shop, "what's up for today."

"We've got tickets for the show tonight, right?" said Leonard Pant.

"Right, but that doesn't start until nine-thirty. What should we do until then?"

"Well," said Mink, pulling a brochure from his shirt pocket, "there are a few things I'd like to see while we're out here."

Leonard looked at the paper, "Museums? You've got a list of museums?"

"I thought they'd be fun," said Mink.

Leonard, Louis, Mink and I studied the offerings. Rusty wasn't paying attention. Three of the girls from the school group had come in for coffee. They were just dressed in tee shirts and shorts and looked pretty tired, but Rusty was still looking. "Too bad," he said, "in a few years those girls will dress up real nice."

We decided which of the places on Mink's list we'd like to go to. His first choice was The Concours Auto Collection and Museum. We all liked cars so that one was easy. He also wanted to see The Western Museum of Kitchen and Bath Fixtures. Mink is in wholesale plumbing. We vetoed that one. Instead we agreed on The Museum of the Very Weird and to keep Rusty interested, we added the Lingerie Museum. Then we'd get lunch, go back to the motel for a swim and a shower, and then to the show.

The auto museum was very cool. I found an old Firebird in the same color as one I'd had years ago. Rusty and Leonard were fascinated by the current estimated values listed on each car's placard. Louis spent a fair amount of time on his back, studying the suspension on a Lotus racecar and Mink just loved everything.

The lingerie museum was located alongside the Victor of Vegas Intimate Wear Shop. That was one of the places I wished Tangee was with me. We have a regular delivery of the Victor of Vegas catalog and she is a frequent buyer. Considering that Rusty hadn't cared much about the museum idea, he sure enjoyed this one. "Damn," he said, looking at one of the more structured bras of the fifties, "you'd have to be a mechanic to get that one off. And that pointy one over there could put your eye out." I told him I supposed that in nineteen-fifty you weren't supposed to get your eyes all that close to a woman's breast. To be fair, we all liked Victor of Vegas, and I got a start on buying souvenirs for Tangee. I thought she'd like the things I bought at Victor's a whole lot better than a, "DO IT IN THE DESERT," tee shirt.

Next up was the Museum of the Very Weird, but since it was past noon we decided to get lunch first.

"Someplace different," said Louis. "No fast food. No place like we've got at home." We consulted the yellow pages and settled on the Jungle Café.

The Jungle Café was out Tropicana Boulevard, about half way to the airport, but with the five of us splitting cab fare it didn't cost too much. The building was all dressed up on the outside with palm trees and tall grasses and tiki torches. Inside it was really nice with nets and carved African masks and maps of the Amazon hanging from the walls. They didn't seem too picky as to which jungle they were talking about.

We ordered drinks while we checked out the menu. My rum and coke had a little monkey holding an umbrella. I put it in my pocket for Tangee because I knew she'd think it was cute. I also put it in my pocket so no one would think I was having a cute drink. I probably should have gotten a beer.

"Whoa!" said Louis. "This is the right place all right. Check it out…they've got ostrich and they've got shark and they've got buffalo."

"And squirrel," said Leonard Pant. "I wonder if they have real food too."

Rusty said, "I saw this movie once about a Japanese restaurant, where they took this live monkey and…"

"I don't want to hear any live monkey stories, Rusty," I said.

"No, really," he went on, "they took this monkey…"

"Rusty, I've heard the live monkey story before when I wasn't getting ready to eat. I didn't like it much then and I sure don't want to hear it now."

He went back to reading the menu. "They got snake," he said.

"Can you really eat turtles?" asked Mink.

Our waiter came back. "The turtle soup is very good," he said. He lowered his voice. "Actually, we used to serve monkey here. And zebra," his eyes darted around.

Rusty started paying attention. "Giraffe?" he asked.

The waiter nodded slightly.

"Man, I'd love to eat some giraffe. Do you…ah…could you still…?"

"No. Not any more," he paused. "PETA. You've heard of them? They picket places if they think animals are being hurt or some such BS. Darn near closed us down. The manager had to agree to not serve anything except regular domesticated animals."

"Ostrich?" asked Mink.

"Yup. There's a couple of ostrich farms within an hour or two of here. Buffalo too. That's very good." Leonard Pant made a face. The waiter said, "I bet you can't tell it from real good, lean beef." Leonard, Mink, Louis and I all got the buffalo burger. Rusty got the ostrich, but I could tell he had giraffe on his mind. Or maybe monkey. I made a mental note to send a thank you note to PETA.

The buffalo tasted good, but maybe a little dry at first. Ketchup and a little hot sauce fixed that. We took a cab back to the motel. As we rode Rusty burped a happy little burp and said, "Man, I ate me an ostrich."

We spent some time at the motel pool. Rusty was making conversation with a few of the schoolgirls. They had sweet young faces with no makeup and just looked cute as hell in their jogging suits. Then they all said how nice it was talking and got up to go to their rooms. "Dang," said Rusty, "do you think they have to study even when they're on vacation?"

We had a few beers and even swam a few times. An hour later Rusty said, "Oh, my God, look at that."

A half-dozen of the most beautiful women I'd ever seen in my life came strolling by the pool. A few wore skintight hip hugging jeans and halter-tops. The others had on very short mini dresses with low cut necklines. Their make-up was perfect and their jewelry was expensive. One of them waved.

"Bye bye, you guys, we got to go. Our flight leaves pretty soon." It was the youngest of the schoolgirls, Christi. She was fourteen. Now she was twenty.

"Wow," said Leonard Pant. "Wow," said Louis. "What?" said Rusty.

"I felt kind of bad," said Christi, "telling you we were from that school and everything. But when we're staying here it's really best that we don't tell people much."

"Like what don't you like to tell?" asked Rusty.

"That we were on a kind of working vacation. See, we're all from Houston, and we all work at different clubs there. You know, gentlemen's clubs? But a few times a year we like to come out here and vacation and see the sights and go to some shows and have some fun. And then we work in one of the clubs here in town for some extra cash."

"Which club?" asked Rusty, his voice deflating.

"This time we were at Club Heaven. It's just that when we're hanging around the motel, we kind of don't like to talk shop. But it was real fun anyway, huh?"

They said goodbyes and walked away, carrying their duffel bags and pulling their little wheeled suitcases.

"How about that? This whole time we were here we've been living with a bunch of strippers and never even knew it," said Mink.

"Yeah. Rusty, how come you didn't pick up on that?" asked Leonard.

"I don't know," said Rusty. "I just don't know." He sounded like a guy who'd just missed a two-foot putt. "I was really fooled. They looked so young. Dang. Well, I'll make up for it." He sounded determined. "This is Las Vegas, Nevada, and before we leave here, I'm going to show you guys how to have a good time."

We left the pool and got showered and ready to go to the show. It was still plenty early, but that would give us a chance to gamble for a while.

Mike Chancey's Casino was one of the older places in Las Vegas and everything was a little smaller than most of the places on the strip. But still it had a nice feeling to it; kind of homey in a glittery, golden, plush, loud, tacky worn out kind of way. We gambled for a bit and then made our way to the theater.

We were seated at a tiny table just off the right aisle, about halfway back from the stage. "We get free drinks, right?" asked Rusty. I checked our ticket stubs and said, "Yeah, we each get two drinks, either a Margarita or a Strawberry Daiquiri."

"Can't we just get beers?" asked Louis.

"I guess if we want something different, we have to pay," I said.

"Then I'm drinking Margaritas," said Rusty. "I'll be damned if I'll pay for a beer when I can get something for free. Do you see a waitress?"

I said, "It looks like we go back to the bar and pick them up there." There was a long line trailing away from a small bar at the rear of the room, but there weren't that many people in it. Wheelchairs and walkers take up a lot of space. The couple in front of us were probably in their seventies. He had on a tan western cut jacket and a cowboy hat. He also wore a bolo tie with a silver and turquoise clasp. His walker had turquoise inlayed down the legs and a pair of miniature steer horns mounted on the cross bar. His wife was wearing electric blue tights and a snug blue sequined top. She was only about twenty pounds overweight so the effect wasn't as bad as it might have been. She had lots of jewelry that looked like silver, but I bet it was platinum. I wished I'd brought my camera. Tangee would have admired her style. The man grumbled about the wait.

"Morris," said his wife, "it's not that bad."

"It's not like at the El Grecco, that's for damn sure," he answered.

"You've been to the El Grecco?" I asked.

"Last time we came out, that's where we stayed," she said.

"We try to make it out two or three times a year, but this kind of slowed us down," Morris tapped at his walker. "I had to stay home last spring to get this knee replaced." He wiggled his right leg.

"It was the other one this year," said his wife.

"Damn it, Madge, it's my knee, and I sure as hell ought to know which one I had fixed."

"It was the other one," said Madge. "Last year it was the right one. Year before that it was your right hip."

"Hmmm," said Morris. "Maybe."

I wondered if I was looking at Tangee and me a few decades down the road. I'd probably loose track of my limbs and she'll sure as heck be wearing sequins. We got our drinks and went back to the table.

We'd all got Daiquiri's or Margarita's except for Louis, who got a beer.

"Damn fool to be buying drinks when you can get them for free," said Rusty.

Then we tasted our drinks. My strawberry Daiquiri was a lot like a cross between oily, fermented, red pop and half-frozen cough syrup. From the looks on their faces, the other guy's Margarita's were about the same. Through tight lips Rusty said, "At least they're free." Louis sipped his Budweiser and smiled. The house lights went down and the show started.

A very large man dressed in a tuxedo came on to the stage, and I recognized him. Many years ago he had been a professional wrestler, Wubba the Clown. I'd seen him on TV. Now he seemed to be the Master of Ceremonies. He told a few lame jokes and made his famous, "wubba, wubba, wubba," sound that he used to make when he put his opponents in his patented headlock and stuffed cotton candy in their mouths so they couldn't fight back.

Then he introduced the first act, the comic, MelView Washington, which was a nice surprise since I'd thought MelView Washington was long dead. My dad used to have MelView Washington party records that he'd play for his friends. His big comedy specialty was referring to body parts by funny names and insulting people. He started his routine with a number of stupid, dated jokes about airline food and answering machines. The old people in the audience laughed, so there was a lot of laughing.

He talked about tits and he talked about penises and he talked about vaginas. He compared breasts to every kind of fruit you could think of. They were melons and tomatoes and pears…a pair of pears, he said. Penises were hoses and sausages and ball peen hammers. He was more creative about vaginas: whirligigs, snack cakes, boiler rooms, front porches. It seemed that any word that came into his head he used as a body part. He said things like, "…and oh, yeah, he sure gonna use his ball peen hammer to rectify her front porch," and, "Shoot, with a crocus like hers, he sure gonna wanna plant his daffodil." Most of it didn't make much more sense than that, but the old people laughed. Rusty laughed, too. The rest of us chuckled, maybe because if we didn't it would mean that we didn't know what it meant to rectify a snack cake, and we sure as hell knew as much about rectifying as anybody. MelView concluded by reminding the women to keep their whirligigs spinning or their men would be putting their drumsticks in somebody else's pistachio bowl.

Then Wubba introduced, "One of the greatest shows in America or any other continent. A show that the Las Vegas Review of Downtown Shows and Sights called, 'Real Good.'"

A strobe light started strobing and ten or twelve people came onto the stage, moving in time to a heavy, syncopated beat coming from some giant speakers. They were all women of different ages and they started doing acrobatics and tumbles. They swayed and rocked, jumping through flaming hoops and waving streamers.

"Damn," said Louis, "that one looks just like Cher. Except I don't think Cher's shoulders are anywhere near that wide."

I showed Louis the show program that had been propped up on the table. "Ah, Louis," I said, "that's because this Cher is a guy. They're all guys."

"No," said Louis.

"Yup," I said, "all of them."

Just then the one dancer who looked like Dolly Parton quit dancing and stepped to the center of the stage where she took off her beaded, low cut top.

"No," said Louis. "That's no man."

I showed him the playbook.

"I'll be damned," he said.

"I'll be damned," said Rusty. "That's one big bunch of silicone."

"Two, actually," I suggested. He nodded. The Dolly impersonator danced and jiggled for a little while and then Cher took off her top. Quite amazing.

"So who are the others supposed to be?" asked Mink.

"Well," said Leonard Pant, who was having a hard time taking his eyes off Cher, "I'd guess that blonde might supposed to be Farrah Faucet, or somebody. The other ones I'm not sure of."

"That one with the black hair looks like that girl who played the alien FBI agent on TV a few years ago," said Mink.

"Some of them look a lot older," said Louis. "That tall one balancing the other two on her shoulders…it could be Margaret Thatcher. Or maybe Hilary Clinton. She's tall. Although the real Hilary Clinton is really much nicer looking than this one."

It was an interesting show, and when it ended with Hilary taking off her top, I was sorry it was over. We all clapped a lot.

Wubba the Clown clapped too, and told a few more stupid jokes as he got ready to introduce the grand finale. The curtains parted, and in front of us was a huge aquarium, all lit with blue and green and yellow. In front of the aquarium were Mishu and Koan, the two world famous Asian magicians. They were wearing headset microphones and I think they introduced each other as they bounced on the balls of their feet, but it was hard to tell because of their accents and some distortion from the microphones. Then they stepped aside and motioned with their arms, gesturing toward the aquarium. From the depths of the water two Great White sharks swam lazily to the front of the tank.

Koan climbed up a ladder and walked out onto a plank suspended over the tank, all the while pulling yard after yard of silk from his mouth. Everyone clapped. Mishu and Koan took turns doing tricks over the tank. Then Koan, having finished balancing some spinning pie plates on a stick over the tank, tossed the plates to Mishu and bowed. Everyone clapped. Koan wobbled and there was a collective gasp from the audience. Then he stood straight. Then he wobbled again and this time made a perfect dive, right into the tank. Everyone went, "Ooooh." He sucked some air from a line near the bottom and went on to pull several yards of silk from his mouth. Mishu jumped in and they both pulled silk. Everyone clapped.

Koan and Mishu emerged from the tank and took their bows after which they announced something we couldn't understand. With the help of a few assistants they stretched a wide white silk sheet over the front of the tank. We could still see the outlines of the sharks. Mishu yelled, "Sakana dishoopeeroo!" Koan yelled, "Sakana dishoopeeroo!" They flapped the sheet three times, screamed and pulled away the fabric. No more sharks. Everyone clapped. Koan and Mishu bowed. Wubba the Clown came on stage and made some sorry jokes about fish sticks. The house lights came up and we filed out.

As we left we saw tables along side the exit hall. MelView Washington was selling his forty-year-old party records. Wubba the Clown was selling autographed pictures of himself in his wrestling outfit. Koan and Mishu's assistants were selling white vinyl sharks for fifty-five dollars each.

We hung around one of the casino's bars for about an hour. Mink started to yawn. Then the rest of us started to yawn…even Rusty. "What the hell's wrong with us? This is Las Vegas and we're out for a good time and it's not even one in the morning yet."

"I think I'm still on Michigan time," said Mink.

"Oh, yeah," said Rusty. "It's what? Four in the morning back home. Okay, hell, we go back and get some sleep. So what? We still have most of our money and at least a full week to go. We'll be fine by tomorrow."

We shared a cab back to the motel and crashed.

Saturday morning the coffee shop was closed due to a toilet problem so we sat in the bus in the motel parking lot eating scrambled eggs and toast. "Mink," I said, "I could use another piece of toast. Is that one ready yet?"

"Almost. It's a little charred on the edge on one side, but it's better than the last one." He held the bread over the open flame of the Coleman with a long handled spatula. He carried it over and dumped it on my plate, next to the eggs, bits of blackened bread shattering as it fell. I didn't mind the burned toast, but we were also out of coffee. I tried to sound cheerful.

"That's okay. I like it well done." I said.

"So," said Rusty, "we've seen some shows and some magic and a bunch of tourist traps. Can we do stuff that I like today?"

"Sure," said Louis, not thinking too clearly before he spoke, "what did you have in mind?"

What did Rusty always have in mind?

"Tits," said Rusty. "And remember that 'all for one' stuff you told me about so that I'd go to the museums with Mink? We all go."

"I liked the museums," said Mink.

"Then that's it. I got a few places in mind already."

I was pretty sure he did.

"Okay," I said. "I'm in for whatever you've got planned, but I've got to get some coffee first."

We packed up the bus and headed west, parking about two blocks off the strip. There was a small restaurant a few doors up and we went in so I could get my caffeine for the morning. We sat at a table outside to watch people.

"Tits," said Rusty. "You've got to understand that appreciating them is both a science and an art."

"And a lust," added Leonard Pant.

"That too," agreed Rusty. "And don't think that makes it a bad thing."

"Tits," I said, starting to wake up, "you see one, you've seen them both."

"Amateur," said Rusty. "I'll show you."

It's easy to study breasts in Las Vegas. You can tell the women who have just arrived from North Dakota or Indiana. They're the ones not wearing tight, form fitting tee shirts and halter-tops yet. After a day or so, they would be.

"Now," said Rusty, "see those two women over there? The one in white and the one in yellow? What do you think?"

"Pretty," said Mink.

"Tits, Mink, tits, what do you think?"

"Pretty," said Mink.

And they were. The white tee was skinny, about twenty and had very nice breasts by my reckoning. The yellow halter was a year or two older and clearly a larger size.

"Now," said Rusty, leaning back, "what you've got to understand is that they are both nice, but they're very different. It's the rib cage. Really. The one in white has this skinny rib cage. Makes her boobs much more obvious and therefore attractive. The yellow one is like…" he paused and surveyed, "a thirty-six D, but see? Her rib cage is bigger. Not fat. Just bigger. What you look for in boobs is the difference between the size of the rib cage and the size of the tits."

We nodded.

"Unless they're humungous…like her." An orange halter walked by, carrying an ice cream cone. Humungous. "Thirty-eight double D…at least. With tits like those, rib cage don't matter."

I wondered how often the orange halter had to go to the chiropractor. I wondered if her shoulders got tired. Or sore.

"Now there's something," said Rusty, motioning with his coffee cup.

A woman walked toward us, high heels, tailored black slacks, dark blue silk blouse. No bra. Obviously. Our heads turned in unison as she passed. A little smile showed as she went by, but her eyes never moved.

"Pretty near perfect," said Louis.

"Yup," said Rusty, "not real, but perfect. Saline, I'd bet. Possibly silicone. Beautiful job."

"How do you know that?" said Mink.

"They didn't move except for that little jiggle when her heels hit the sidewalk."

I got a refill of my coffee and sipped as Rusty made running commentary on the passing women.

"Nice. Ooh, over there, very nice. And there, in the red? Just right…padded bra, but a great effect. Victor's of Las Vegas, the Smooth Intimacies collection, I think. And this one? The one coming toward us? Very small but very nice…see? It's the rib cage." Never once did he have an unkind thing to say about any woman who came into our view.

"But, you know," he went on, "mostly what you see isn't real."

"You think there's that many implants?" asked Louis.

"It's not that…it's the bras. Now don't get me wrong, I love bras. It's just that when a woman wears a bra, the shape of her tits is the shape of the bra. You know damn well that when a woman takes off her bra, she's not the same shape she is when she's got it on. Unless she's like eighteen or something, they either droop or flatten or are pointy or something. It's a rare thing to see a naked, adult woman who still shows a great shape."

I smiled, thought of Tangee and just nodded, smiling to myself.

"Finish your coffee, Buck," this is Las Vegas and we're going to see some perfect tits today. Come on, it's past noon already."

We got back in the bus. "Head back toward the motel," called Rusty from his seat, "and when you get to a big tan factory next to a used car lot, turn right."

Half a block after I turned right I saw a big pink concrete block building with a giant blue X on the roof. "How did you know this was here?" I asked as we parked in the wide gravel driveway.

"Blue X, man, it's world famous. The biggest selection of erotica in the universe. I saw the X when we drove by before."

It cost five dollars to walk in the door. "A store with a cover charge?" asked Mink.

"Think of it as a museum," said Rusty.

The Museum of Modern Sex, I thought. There were a dozen rows, each eighty feet long, with rack after rack of DVDs, some in categories I hadn't ever thought of, and some in categories I wished I hadn't learned about then. A smaller area had thousands of different books and magazines. One whole wall was covered with displays of artificial sex parts as well as accessories for the parts you already have. In one corner was a pair of blow-up sex dolls sitting in a kind of leather swing, suspended from the ceiling. I wondered at how you'd secure it to your ceiling joists and if you'd leave it up all the time in a special room or if you'd only put it up for certain occasions. I guessed when you weren't swinging you could put some hanging flowerpots in it or something.

At the back of the store was a doorway leading to movie peep shows. Louis and I wandered back there and into a dimly lit hallway with several door openings on each side. I stepped into one, put a dollar into the slot and watched three minutes of uninspired intercourse. I left that room and went to another, thinking there might be a better movie in there. Instead, I found a man standing, watching a movie with his pants down around his knees. He smiled at me. I left. The same thing might have happened to Louis, because when I met him at the front counter he was still blushing.

Rusty looked at every single thing in the store and it took an hour and a half to get him out. He left with a pink plastic bag that had a big blue X on it.

"Let's get lunch," said Rusty.

We agreed. Rusty said, "A left out of the driveway and a right on the main street. Go up three traffic lights." At the third traffic light was Tassels, a strip club.

"For lunch?" asked Mink.

"They have a buffet from noon until four. Ribs and everything."

"Really…how do you know this stuff?" I asked.

"I just do,' said Rusty. Uncanny.

The buffet was good. Ribs and everything. There were only four girls working and they took turns on the stage. When they weren't up dancing they retreated to tables where they spoke with guys.

"The guys must be regulars," said Rusty. "Or really big tippers. They'll never come over and dance for us."

"They do that here?" asked Leonard Pant. "Like at Boob's Bar at home?"

"Yeah, they do that here. But not like Boob's Bar. This is Vegas. We got to find a place with more women."

We finished our lunch with Rusty comparing rib cages. Then we left. "Let's try this place I saw in this flyer," said Rusty. "I picked it up at the adult store."

He had a tabloid-sized newspaper with advertisements for what seemed like every strip club in town. He was pointing to an ad for The Strip Mall. Six strip bars in one location. Zoning is different in Las Vegas. I got stuck in some construction traffic and it took nearly forty hot minutes to get there. Rusty said, "We'll start at one end and go all the way through to the other."

I figured I'd have to switch to cokes half way through, but at least I wouldn't have to drive between bars.

The first bar was the Pioneer. The girls all wore cowboy hats. We had a drink and Rusty and Leonard each got a girl to dance at our table for them. Rusty loved it and Leonard even smiled a little. We hit two more of the bars and by then we'd each gotten up-close dances from some of the girls. Louis was getting drunker with each stop and was really loosening up. Rusty got into a conversation with one of the girls and spent the best part of an hour telling her how he was a big shot at General Motors and we were his junior vice presidents and we were all out in Vegas as a bonus for how good a job we did back home. We were spending money so she would have stayed with us anyway, but Rusty just can't not BS around women. He asked her, just like he's asked at least one woman at every bar we'd been to, if she'd like to step out to our deluxe motor home with him for a while. She said no just like all the others had said no.

Rusty said, "Before I'm done tonight, I'm going to have myself one of those dancers."

"But they all say no," said Louis. "Do you think one of them would really go with you? Or me?"

"You're interested too, huh? I thought you would be. Sure, lots of them don't mind making a little money on the side. It's just that they probably can't leave during their shift, or there aren't enough girls working so they can slip out."

We left around nine without a dancer girl for either Louis or Rusty.

"Rusty, this is fun and all, but I don't think I want to do all the rest of these clubs," said Mink.

"Okay," he said. "One more. Then we'll find something else to do. Me and Louis are still going to find us a show girl." I was only little less drunk than the rest of them, and frankly, I didn't care.

The third bar looked just like the others on the outside, but was very different once we stepped in. It was almost totally dark in the entrance hall and I could barely see that there was a cashier's window ahead of us. It slid open and a guy appeared. "ID and ten bucks," he said.

"ID?" said Rusty. "Like we all don't look twenty-one?"

"ID and ten bucks," said the guy.

They all showed him their driver's licenses in their wallets as I fished my license out of my shoe. "No wallet?" he said.

"Yeah," I said.

"Show me."

I wasn't sure what was up, but I showed him. He buzzed a buzzer and let us in.

"Guys," said Rusty, "I think this is the real thing."

This place was even darker than the Beer Bar back home. There was just a red glow along the walls and a few dim lights behind the bar, where we sat down. Out of the dark came two girls. One of them walked up and stood between Mink and me and the other between Rusty and Louis.

"So, you boys making the rounds?" asked the short redhead next to me.

"Yeah, seeing the sights," I said.

I felt her hand on my thigh as she said, "Have you found what you're looking for yet?" Her hand moved further up, until it was almost to my crotch. I could feel her fingernails.

"Well," I said, feeling more than a little nervous, "you never know."

The other girl was doing the same with Louis and Rusty had this huge smile on his face.

"One of you guys like to buy your lady a drink?" It was the same guy who took our money at the door.

"Maybe in a bit," I said.

"I don't know," said Louis, "what would you like to drink?"

Slim blonde next to him moved her hand a little higher on his leg and said, "I kind of like wine. Do you?" Louis drank mostly beer, but he nodded his head, "Wine is nice."

"Split a bottle?" asked the bartender.

"Well…"

"I should mention that if you split a nice bottle of wine with the lady, we have rooms in back where you two could enjoy it in privacy."

Rusty's grin expanded.

By this time, Louis' girl had her hand up right between his legs and was petting him.

"Sure," said Louis. His voice was getting higher.

The bartender disappeared and returned a few minutes later with a wine bottle. He showed it to Louis. "Is this satisfactory?"

Louis nodded.

"Very fine," said the bartender. "just sign for it and I'll show you two to a nice little room.

The bar was so dark I could barely see that he'd put a small receipt slip with a pen in front of Louis. He signed. The bartender worked a corkscrew and poured two glasses.

"Now," he said, "if you'll just pay the three hundred dollars, I'll show you to a room."

It took a second to register. "Three hundred dollars?" said Louis. Even Rusty looked surprised.

"For the wine. Look, you signed for it."

"Three hundred dollars?"

"That's right. And you pay for that up front, before you get a room."

"But…I don't…ah…."

"Now look, I've got a signed receipt. If you've got a problem with that, we can call the police and have them explain about unpaid bar bills. Besides, don't forget that includes the room and…" he nodded at the blonde. "You do have the money?"

"Yeah." Louis pulled three bills from the back of his wallet.

"There. Perfect. Now, if you two will step around here…" and Louis disappeared behind a curtain with the bartender and the girl.

"How about you, honey?" asked my redhead.

"Ah, not just right now," I said. The other guys said the same and she disappeared into the darkness.

When the bartender returned we each bought a ten-dollar beer and sat at a table.

"I told you this would be great," said Rusty. "When he comes back, and we find out all about it, how the rooms are and how the girl was and everything, then I'm going to talk to that little redhead. What about you, Buck?"

"No. But don't let me slow you guys down."

"Leonard?"

"Not in my budget."

"Mink?"

"I'm married, Rusty. Remember?" Rusty rolled his eyes. Mink said, "Hey, just because you're not, don't mean we have to do what you do."

"You weren't too shy about having that naked dancer girl sitting on your lap a few bars back."

"That's different. My wife…she'll understand that." He nodded at the curtained door. "But that's something she wouldn't understand."

"You're going to tell her everything you did out here?"

"Why not? Some gambling and some drinking and looking at naked women…shoot, she expects that. And when I get home I can tell her what a good time I had and not worry about lying. And then we'll go upstairs and get naked and she'll turn out the light."

I thought that that was pretty much how it would go at my house when I got back., except Tangee will leave the light on. She'll believe me and we'll go upstairs and get naked, but she'll leave the light on. You can't check for hickeys in the dark.

A half-hour later, a lot sooner than I expected, Louis came back, holding the wine bottle. "You can't leave with the bottle," called the bartender.

"For three hundred bucks I can," said Louis.

"Don't make me call…" said the bartender, picking up a phone.

Louis poured the last ounce of my ten-dollar beer over the wine bottle label, peeled it off and stuck it in his pocket. He dropped the bottle on the floor. "Let's go," he said.

Rusty had a very confused look on his face, but we all got up and walked out. We stood in a circle in the parking lot next to the bus.

"What happened?" asked Leonard Pant. "Why did we leave?"

"We go back down this hall, me and the blonde," said Louis, looking at the cement, "and the guy opens a door and there's this little tiny room. It's got a bed and a little plastic table. And she sits on the bed, and I sit on the bed, and I'm not quite sure what to do next because I never was with a woman like that before. I mean for money. And she scoots over real close and takes off her top and says, 'So what are you interested in?' I didn't know what to say. I thought, sex, that's what I'm interested in, but she wanted me to be a little more specific. So, finally she said, 'Just regular? Nothing extra or weird?' and I said okay. She starts taking off her G-string and says, 'Okay, that's five hundred to start. If we get into it and you want something extra, we'll see.'"

"Five hundred?" said Rusty, his eyes wide.

"To start," said Louis. "I told her that I didn't have five hundred more dollars on me. I asked about the three hundred-dollar wine and the room and everything. She said that was just for the wine and the room. Anything else between the two of us was separate. Then she asked me how much I did have, and I guessed about three-twenty and she put her top back on and told me she'd drive me to an ATM. I told her I didn't have a cash card. We sat for a few minutes drinking the wine, which wasn't even all that good, I don't think. I told her I was sorry, but everything was turning out different than I thought it would. She was kind of nice about it but I think she was mad."

"So you didn't get anything? Nothing?" asked Rusty. "Not even a naked lap dance."

"Nothing," said Louis. "By the time I left I was sad and mad and frustrated. Here, I'd got myself all talked into spending some money and having a pretty show girl in Las Vegas and having something I could remember for a long time and then, nothing."

We all told him how it wasn't so bad and that it was still kind of fun in a sexually frustrating kind of way; not all that much different from having naked girls squirm on your lap at Boob's Bar.

"Besides," said Rusty, "when we get home, you can always tell people that you went back in that little room and it was the best sex you ever had and not even mention the five-hundred dollar part. We'd back you up. Wouldn't we? I sure would."

Nobody said much.

"Hey, were you guys just in there? Did you get what you were looking for?" It was a short, thin faced guy with sandy blond hair and some kind of accent that wasn't Mexican.

"Well," said Louis, "I sure got screwed."

"Is that so? Now, I had heard that that place was nothing but a scam." He sounded European. We later learned he was Russian.

"Yeah," said Louis. "An expensive one."

"Ah. So you didn't get screwed, you got screwed."

We nodded.

"Still looking for something?"

Rusty's eyes lit up. Nobody else's did. Rusty said, "What do you got going on?"

"I still got a few seats left for the real show." The Russian guy spent a lot of time looking over his shoulder. "You want in?"

"For what?" asked Leonard Pant.

"Live show. The real thing. No phoney-ass club. No scam. Live show ten feet in front of you. It only goes down once a night and I only got room for ten guys total. I got six already but I'll make room for you five."

"How much?" said Rusty.

"A hundred bucks. Worth every penny. It's this real cute girl and her boyfriend. He's real...tall. And before their show there's a bunch of cute girls who do a little strip show. A hundred bucks. And after the show, some of the girls will, you know, go with you for a while."

"How much for that?"

"Most of them get like fifty for a little something. A hundred would get you anything you wanted. That's between you and them."

"I've heard that before," said Louis.

"At least this is up front," said Rusty. "Let's do it."

"Shoot," said Mink, "I'm tired and I don't care much to see this."

"Then close your eyes," said Rusty. "Come on, we've gone this far. And poor Louis, we got to go just for him, anyway. Poor frustrated guy. Come on. What's another hundred bucks? And if me and Louis spend a little more later on, you guys can wait in the bus."

"But," said Louis to the little Russian, "No money up front."

"Okay, not here. But when we get to the house. You're not going to see the show and then not have any money. Show me now you got the cash and I'll take you there. When you see the show is for real, you pay."

Everybody showed him the cash was, indeed, in their wallets and he said, "Follow the little white car," and he pointed to a tired, dented Kia sedan. Not much profit in live sex shows, I thought. "And when we get there, park down on the next block. Behind the party store. Don't want to call too much attention to the house. You know."

I think he was surprised when we got in the bus, but he got in his tiny car and waved his arm to follow. It was an easy ten minutes to a darkly lit residential neighborhood of small frame houses. I parked on the street next to the party store and we walked up to where our new friend stood on the sidewalk. He took us in and we were shown to a good sized back bedroom that had its closet knocked out to make more space. A second doorway had been made in a side wall and was covered with a blanket.

Four men were there already, standing against a wall. There were no chairs and we stood too. A queen-sized bed on the other side of the room was the only furniture and it was lit by a few track lights mounted in the ceiling. There was a rope stretched across the room to keep us on our side. We were joined by a massive man in jeans and a skin tight tee shirt. The bouncer. "Money," he said. We all counted out our money into his big, flat hand. Then he stepped back.

He flicked a switch and the regular lights went out and two of the track lights came on. I heard a click and music started from a CD player I'd missed when we came in.

Three women walked into the room through the blanket door. One hissed something over her shoulder and a fourth girl came in. The two shortest stood on the bed and the taller ones were on the floor and they moved to the music. After one song they took off their tops and danced some more. They were not skinny but not fat either: not pretty and not plain. Their smiles often slipped. The Russian man moved through us with glasses. "Ten bucks. Tequila. Half a glass." We paid.

The women took off their shorts and then their G-strings. During the last song they touched each other and one pair kissed for a moment. Then three of them left and the one remaining lay on the bed and got intimate with a few sex toys. We'd all crowded close to the rope.

The song ended, the music stopped and the girl left.

The Russian guy came in past the blanket and told us the main show would start right after the next song. While it played, Rusty whispered to me, "That last one…the brunette…when this is over, I'm going to see about getting with her."

"Okay," I said, "You know where the bus is."

The guy came through again with the bottle and we all got refills. They were small glasses.

New music came on and the lights all went red. A girl wearing a black dress came in and curled up on the bed. Then a naked man walked in. The show lasted about thirty minutes. He was very tall. We strained at the rope to see.

The couple was right in the middle of everything when the Russian burst in and yelled, "Is being busted! Oh shit! Is being a bust!"

There was a terrible trample of people out of the bedroom. I called, "Guys…there's a back door through the kitchen." We ran through the doorwall and scrambled across the small backyard and vaulted the low concrete fence. We crossed several backyards and fences and finally moved to the sidewalk, running toward the corner where the bus was parked. I jumped in and started the motor with

Rusty right behind me. Louis was a few seconds after that and a minute later Leonard Pant and Mink puffed up to the door. I put the bus in drive and turned right at the first corner. I found a street that looked familiar and took a left. I tried hard not to speed; I had way too much beer and tequila in me to get stopped.

Five quiet minutes of driving later, Leonard Pant said, "My wallet. It's gone."

There was a lot of cussing. Everyone's wallet was gone.

"We're going back!" yelled Rusty.

"No, we're not," I said.

"Oh, yeah. We're going back."

"All those guys, Rusty…they were probably in on it. The guys in the kitchen, the Russian, the bouncer, for sure. Even the women. We'd get our asses whipped."

"Then the police. We'll call them."

"And say what? 'Well, yes officer, that's about it…we were at this live sex show and hoping to score with some prostitutes, and we got ripped off.' Right."

I kept driving.

We got back to the motel and counted our remaining assets. I still had my driver's license a credit card and a few hundred dollars cash in my shoe. Mink had eighty-three dollars in the nightstand and Louis had sixty dollars in chips from the casino. Leonard Pant and Rusty had carried almost all of their money in their wallets. We had less than that when we checked out of the motel Sunday morning.

We couldn't afford breakfast and probably couldn't have held it down anyway. Beer and tequila and wine from the night before had created a five-person hangover that meant sunny side up eggs were out of the question. We packed the bus and headed toward the freeway, driving slowly. The morning was cool and the sky was sweet but we didn't really notice.

"Buck," said Mink, "there's a church up ahead on the right. Pull in the parking lot."

I thought he had to barf. Instead he said, "Shut the bus down. We're going in here."

Leonard Pant and Rusty started to object. Louis, his head in his hands, didn't say anything. "Last night we did your thing, Rusty. It's my turn. Come on." Too sick to argue and possibly in need of an indoor bathroom, they followed. I helped Louis.

The church was pretty good sized; about fifteen pews and a wide center aisle. Up in front the wall was covered with bright white texturized paint troweled into overlapping semicircles and embedded with millions of sparkles. The cross that hung there was about eight feet high, covered with silver sequins and lit up by some track lights in the ceiling. Tangee would have loved it. There was a white wooden stand where the preacher was reading from his notes about the pancake breakfast next week and the building fund. Behind him was a young girl at an electric piano keyboard and about six other people who I figured were the choir.

There were a fair number of people at the service and the five of us had to sit in two different pews. Rusty, Mink and Leonard Pant sat behind Louis and me. We drew a lot of funny looks from the congregation and it occurred to me that five unshaved, disheveled, hungover guys are more than five times more obvious than one.

We had just settled in when we had to get up again because it was time to sing. I believe that the sound level would have been loud even if we hadn't been hung over, but in my sensitive state, the music didn't even seem to come in through my ears…it cut a direct route through my skull to the center of my brain. Also, when the music started, we found that the folks on the platform behind the preacher weren't the choir, they were the band. I'd seen church bands with Tangee in her church before, but Louis is a Lutheran, and from the look on his face, they don't have saxophones at his church. Also, probably not a bass guitar, a lead guitar, a trumpet and a drum kit. They had an overhead projector lit up to show the words to the songs on a screen, with was good because I didn't know any of them. They all had a kind of modern, pop sound to them, and I know that Tangee's momma would have walked right out since they didn't start with "The Old Rugged Cross." Several people had pastel streamers that they waved in time to the music, about eight had tambourines and two women in front looked like they were using sign language along with the words.

The first song lasted fifteen minutes. It was called, "Oh, Sweet Jesus, Worthy of Praise; We fight the Enemy all of our Days." The title was also the first two lines of the song and it was sung over and over again about eighty times. Then the next few lines were sung and then back to the beginning for another five minutes. I guessed it was supposed to focus our minds on Sweet Jesus, but I found my brain rooting around trying to find something else to think about. The five of us mumbled our way through four or five songs and then we got to sit down. I didn't think this was quite what Mink had in mind.

The Reverend Robert J. Partch began to speak; low and soft, in a voice that sounded like a cross between velvet and STP.

"It's a *good day*," began the preacher. "It's a *good day* to be right with the Lord."

A reedy woman two rows back shouted, "Yes, Lord. Tell it, Reverend."

He smiled, "A *good day*. With the Lord. You know," he looked out over the congregation, "there's people who think a *good day* is a day when they can make a lot of money. Or it's a *good day* when they can drive their brand new white Mercedes Benz 500SE down the road. Or it's a *good day* when their numbers hit at keno or their slots all show sevens or their cards come up twenty-one." He walked away from the speaker's stand and kept talking, his voice rising a little every time he said the words, "Good day." "Some people think it's a *good day* because they've got a new bottle of liquor. Or a case of beer. Or a package of mar-i-juana. Or some cocaine…or crack…or heroin…or some or another of whatever kind of narcotic they can get their hands on."

He was talking a lot faster now, and the faster he spoke the more of a southern accent he got. "But those things are not the things of Gawd. They are not the things of Jee-ah-sus. You know…those things are the things of SATAN! Of the DEVIL!"

There were a lot of "Amens" and "Halleluiahs." Robert J. Partch had taken off his French Vanilla Ice Cream colored suit jacket and loosened the collar of his cranberry colored shirt. His face was getting shiny. Louis just stared at him. Pastor Partch had somehow moved on to the subject of dirt.

"…and the Lord won't have no dirty feet in heaven. And no sin-dirtied hands are gonna get an answer if they go knocking on the Pearly Gates of Heaven. And there's gonna be no feet that walked in sin that get to walk the golden streets. Gawd won't have it. Gawd won't have it! GAWD…WON'T…HAVE…IT!!!" He was at the edge of the stage or platform or altar and he was springing up and down on his toes at the end of every sentence as he preached. He pulled a cranberry colored handkerchief from a back pocket and started blotting the sweat that was beading on his forehead. He dropped to one knee, as if to catch his breath. He lowered his head. Then he held out his left arm and pointed to the front row.

A strikingly beautiful woman stood up. She was about thirty-five and had on a long navy dress. She was turned half to the preacher and half to the congregation. She held her folded hands near her throat and started to shake. Her eyes were closed. She spoke, too quiet to hear at first, but then louder. "Shala meecon. Shala meecon halawa. Masteen chalanga meecon. Collowa asteer butin."

Louis nudged me, "What…?"

"Tongues," I said. "She's talking in tongues. They believe it's the actual voice of God going right through her. In His own language. Really."

A short round woman stood and started filling in the spaces every time the other woman took a breath. I guessed she was translating.

"Kallenestro itsa palaua meecon tua."

"Your God knows the sins of Man."

"Meecon shawala beeook."

"I know that Man is tempted and falls to sin."

"Rantellora pedestrum meesik shalikum."

"And that Man must repent and…"

I looked over at Louis and he had his eyes square on the woman speaking in God's voice. He was swaying a little but I figured that had more to do with last night's tequila than any spiritual spirits.

After a few minutes the pretty woman collapsed flat on the floor. She just kind of crumpled. The short round woman started to sing and three churchwomen left their seats and fanned the fainted lady with folded church programs. In a few seconds she came to, smiled and stood up.

The Reverend Partch was standing in the aisle preaching about the power of God when a pudgy teenaged girl stood up and held her hugely fat baby out to him. Partch shouted prayers and the baby screamed and the mother mumbled a continuous stream of "praise Jesus and Hallelujah." She sat back down and Partch advanced two steps, pointing at an elderly man with a scruffy beard.

The man stood and Partch, his voice rising and falling like a high wind in winter, called the Holy Spirit to come into this man and shrink his tumor. He yelled at the devil to leave his body. Partch jumped and pointed and walked completely around the man, praying and singing and sometimes saying unintelligible words. Then he stood in front of him, rose up on his toes and reached out, touching the sick man's forehead with his thumb and forefinger. The man stiffened like a steel rod and fell forward into the pastor's arms. Three ushers helped him to his seat.

And then Pastor Partch came to us. He pointed at Louis with his right hand and to the aisle with his left. His eyes were absolutely black and unblinking. Sweat had soaked through his cranberry colored shirt. His whole body was quivering. Louis stepped in front of me and stood in front of the preacher. He looked exhausted with his back slumped a little and his hands loose at his sides.

Partch stood on his tiptoes and was still a good four inches shorter than Louis. Then, quicker than a karate move, his right arm shot out and he grabbed Louis' forehead in his hand. He turned to face the right side of the congregation and shouted, "The prodigal son!" Then, to Louis in a softer voice, "Brother, you're home. You didn't know it when you came in here and I didn't know that you were coming here, but you're home. God brought you to this place." With his right hand still gripping Louis' forehead, he grasped his shoulder with the other, "Tell me your pain. Tell God your pain."

Louis was quiet.

"Say it, Brother, say the words. Tell me your pain."

Louis mumbled, "I have a headache."

"Of course you have a headache! And you know why. It's the Devil. He knows what you've been up to, just like God knows, but the devil made you do things and put the pain in your head so you couldn't hear the word of God. But God is mighty!" Partch released Louis and gestured. The woman in the navy dress and her short, round friend and two other women from the front row walked up the aisle. Together with Pastor Partch they surrounded Louis, linked arms in a circle and closed in on him, making a giant group hug. Then Partch started preaching again and the navy dress woman started speaking in tongues. The other three traded amens and hallelujahs, and in unison, the group of them began to bounce on their toes. Louis had to start bouncing just to keep up.

I was getting kind of worried that with all the liquor from last night and all the weird food we'd eaten, Louis was about to barf, which might have really spoiled the church service. Or maybe not...I don't know what a real exorcism is like and maybe Partch would have figured it was just the devil getting chased out of Louis. Anyway, after a few more minutes the jumping stopped and they all stood back and sang a song and they all kneeled down right in the aisle and Louis knelt down with them and they prayed. Then they stood up and Partch patted Louis' back and the ladies hugged him one more time and Louis came back to his seat, which he fell into like he'd just run a marathon.

Partch made his way back to the altar, pausing briefly to cure a bad case of psoriasis and a small tumor. The congregation sang one more song and started filtering out. We didn't talk at all until we got back to the bus.

We left the church parking lot and I found a MacDonalds. I needed coffee. We sat as far away from the screaming kids at the indoor playground as we could and stared into our cups.

"Well, Mink, we found you a church," I said. "Was that quite what you were looking for?"

He looked up at me, "Not exactly, but it was okay."

"You like all that whooping and hollering?" asked Leonard Pant.

"I like it quieter, but it's all right. I just thought I wanted to be in some church after last night."

"What kind of church do you usually go to?" I asked.

"Usually I don't. Sometimes I do. I'll just drive along and if I see a church without too many cars in the parking lot, I'll go in. I like quiet ones best. Sometimes I'll go to one of the hospitals and go to the little chapels they have there."

"And you pray in there?"

"Not exactly. I mean, I don't have special words or I don't have prayers memorized or anything. I just kind of let it sink in. Hard to explain."

"I was raised Catholic," said Rusty.

"No kidding?" said Mink.

"Yeah. What, you don't think I look like a Catholic or something? It was kind of nice. Always mostly the same. Real dignified. I think like some of these new religions, it's like they're making fun of God."

"New religions?" I asked. "Like those new-fangled Baptists?"

"Yeah. Like them, and all those like the one we just went to, where they're yelling and crying and everything. I bet God laughs his butt off about them," said Rusty.

"And God doesn't think the Pope is funny with that pointed hat? I mean, no offence, but be careful what you're calling weird," said Mink.

"It doesn't matter," I said. "I don't think it hurt us one bit to be in a church after last night."

"Hey," said Leonard, "last night wasn't all that sinful. I've had nights a whole lot wilder than that. But Louis, man, they sure had your number. And you went along with it. I couldn't hardly believe it, you jumping and praying and crying."

"I don't know," said Louis, "he just pointed at me and it was like I had to do it. Was I crying?"

Leonard said, "Yeah, I just couldn't believe it, you in the middle of all that Holy Roller bull shit, and going along with it too. I thought you had more sense. Geez…'Tell me your pain,' I thought I'd die."

That sounded pretty rude. "Hey, come on, Leonard."

"What, you think God is going to zap me? Prayers and miracles…you guys are too much. So, Louis, did you get your miracle?"

"I think, maybe. My headache is gone."

"Oh, geez. Maybe you should get down on your knees and thank Saint Tylenol. You took enough of them before we even got there. What crap."

We got back to the bus and I hopped on northbound I-15.

Mink said, "You don't go to church, do you Leonard?"

"Never," he answered. "Except for weddings and funerals and stuff like that. Not since I was a kid and my dad would slap me stupid if I didn't."

"So you didn't like it because you had to go?"

"No. I didn't like it because it was stupid."

"I never thought it was stupid," said Mink quietly.

"Hey, okay, here's the deal," said Leonard. "I was like five years old and we're going to this church down the block from the house. And every Sunday about half way through, all us little kids had to leave. There had been singing and the minister had made some announcements and there'd been some praying, and then us kids would have to leave and go downstairs to the youth rooms. It pissed me off. They were just getting to the good stuff and I had to leave.

"I knew just what they were doing, too. I figured once the kids were out, they got down to the real magic. They passed around the secrets about God and probably He appeared at the altar and talked to them and showed them miracles and slide shows of what heaven looks like and everything. They just figured we were too little to understand so they got us out of the way. And then, when you were old enough, you got confirmed and you started learning the magic and the secrets and could stay upstairs and talk to God.

"I hated going downstairs with some poor old woman or some teenager. We had to cut whales out of blue paper and then paste little paper men inside them, like Jonah. And while we pasted and cut, they'd tell us these lame-ass stories about Jonah and how he got swallowed by a whale. Or we'd have to line up all these plastic animals on the deck of this plastic boat while we heard about how Noah rounded up two of all the animals…well, shit you know the story.

"So, here we were, listening to these baby stories while upstairs God is doing magic. And then, one Sunday, I couldn't take it any more. I must have been about seven or eight. While all the kids and the Sunday school teachers were busy, I snuck out. I went to the church. Then I found some stairs that went up to where the choir was and I found a place were I could hide and still see and hear what was going on down in the church. And you know what was going on down there? Well, it sure as hell wasn't God putting on a slide show. No magic. No secrets. You know what the minister was preaching to the congregation about? Jonah and the freaking whale! It was the same stupid children's' story that they told downstairs! I couldn't believe it. I couldn't believe it.

"Time went on and I found out that that's all church is about, is forgetting every reasonable, intelligent thing you ever learned, and depending on a religion based on fairy tales.

"I think I cried then and I want to cry now, hearing you say that some shrimp in a purple shirt with 'Pastor' in front of his name made your headache go away. Remember what I said about Saint Tylenol."

"I need more coffee."

Nobody talked. Not for miles. Even Rusty quit shouting when he saw a pretty woman. He didn't quit looking, but he did quit shouting.

I just drove. A few times I tried to get the purple orangutan out of the seat adjuster gears so somebody else could drive, but he wouldn't budge. We would have had to take the whole seat mechanism apart, and I was pretty sure we'd never get it put together right. Utah passed quietly, which I guess is what Utah does anyway.

Louis had done the math and figured that with the cash we had left, we'd just be able to afford gas for the return trip, if we camped every night and cooked our own food. Leonard Pant had made a few calls about getting a replacement for one of his credit cards or a cash advance against it, but he learned it would take days to work it out. His card company was based in the Cayman Islands.

Of course, I still had my credit card in my shoe, but I didn't want anybody to know about that, because if they did we'd be staying in nice motels and eating at nice restaurants and buying souvenirs and it would take me four months to itemize everything when the bills came in and longer than that to collect.

We stopped at a small town just before the Colorado border to pick up supplies, and found a place best described as a general store. About half of the place was dedicated to hunting and fishing supplies and the rest to groceries and souvenirs. The sporting goods seemed to account for most of the business because that stuff wasn't dusty. The canned potatoes were.

I gave the guys some money and went back to the bus. It was funny, but after all the driving I'd done, I felt like I wanted to sit down for a while. I set my recliner half way back and dozed while the guys shopped.

The bus door accordioned open and they rustled in with a few large paper bags.

"What did you get?" I asked.

"Mostly canned stuff," said Louis. "They didn't have any fresh produce and the meat looked kind of iffy. We got some hamburger, though, and a couple of packs of hot dogs that weren't past-dated."

"Some iffy hamburger?"

"No. It's the kind they sell in a tube and it had a date on it, too, so I thought it would be okay."

"Was there any change?" I asked.

"Here," Louis handed me four dollars and a few coins. "Prices were a little high, but it would have cost more in gas money to find a cheaper place. But the canned potatoes were cheap."

It was getting late so Mink found a state campground on the map and we headed there. It was a small, very non-deluxe camping place, but that was okay. Mink grilled the hot dogs on an outdoor fire while Louis heated up a few cans of beans on the Coleman. We ate, played cards for an hour or so and went to bed. About four in the morning it started to rain. It didn't seem to bother anybody else, but it woke me up. Really, it didn't bother me much either, but some part of my brain kept trying to figure out the patterns in the raindrops as they splashed on the roof of the bus from an overhanging tree branch. Near dawn I thought I heard a kind of syncopated waltz and I fell back to sleep listening to that. The next morning, since we had practically nothing to pack, we were on the road early, right after my coffee.

By noon we'd driven out from under the rain, but the clouds sat in my rearview mirror all day, chasing us east. That night we camped in a crummy, flat little campsite with no trees and the rain caught us again. The wind was blowing pretty good and we had some leaks around two of the windows. We didn't care. One more night after this and we'd be home. After a half-hearted card game we watched the evening news and went to bed with the bus rocking in the gusty wind.

I was very tired of driving and the next morning we spent a good half-hour trying to get the orangutan out of the seat adjuster gears. We only managed to rip part of him out, leaving the stuck part still stuck. I drove again. The good part was that during the night the storm had taken a right turn and the sky was fresh and clear. The road steamed in the morning sun and the tires hissed. We made good time to our last camping stop of the trip. We stopped at a grocery store and bought a sliced quarter pork loin and five great big potatoes for dinner. I couldn't afford steaks but I couldn't stand another hot dog or hamburger.

We paid for our campsite and set up for the evening. The chops made a beautiful grease fire over the outdoor grill and the potatoes baked in the coals. Mink found a few cans of corn behind the rain ponchos so we actually had a full meal.

The campsite was perfect with its roadways curving in and out between stands of trees. There was a man-made pond with a diving raft in the middle and pontoon paddleboats to rent. Sunset was pink and green and purple and stayed bright for a long time. While there was still some light I said, "I'm going to take a walk." Leonard Pant surprised me and said, "I'll come too." I never though of Leonard as the kind of guy who would take a walk just for the heck of it. Mink came too.

It was less of a walk than a stroll. We weren't going anywhere except just around the park and we took our time. People nodded to us as they walked past. We nodded back. From a hundred feet away I heard, "Jimmy! Jimmy? Come on." Thirty seconds later a ten-year-old in a swimsuit with a towel over his shoulder zipped by on his bike. A young couple stepped out of a nice travel trailer and sat on a pair of lawn chairs under an awning. As we passed I saw the back of their camper had a sign, "Just Married."

Some of the campers had apparently been there for quite a while; maybe all summer. Leonard pointed to one camper's "front yard." They'd built a grotto out of crushed limestone and had a plaster Virgin Mary standing in the middle, sheltered by a half-buried, upended bathtub. We saw at least three other Marys in shrines of different sizes and décor, one of them illuminated with a string of blue Christmas lights. There was also one Buddha and a Lincoln Memorial. Probably at least a third of the sites had pink flamingos and plaster bunnies. One had a plaster Cupid pissing into a shallow pool. Tangee would have loved the place and it made me sad I couldn't be walking with her instead of Leonard Pant and Mink. I could just hear her commenting on the relative beauty of lighted Chinese lanterns versus lighted Tiki torches. I wished my cell phone hadn't died. It was funny. Like, the closer I got to home, the more I missed her. Miles don't matter for that kind of thing…time does.

Rusty went to bed early but the rest of us stayed up until after one, just dealing a few hands of cards, but mostly talking low about things that don't matter much. Then we slept.

The next morning I was eager to get going. I figured that if the weather stayed clear and I didn't make any wrong turns and we didn't make any stupid stops along the way, we could be home by six o'clock that evening. We were right on track, too, until Rusty saw the sign and said, "Look, 'Fireworks-2 miles.' Hey, the Fourth of July is in just a few days." I am a sucker for fireworks.

We pulled into a muddy bowling alley parking lot, parked and walked over to a small circus style tent with its side open. There were card tables all along one side and a blue cargo van behind them. I started strolling past the tables and found the prices were a whole lot less than I remembered paying other years.

Every year since I've been an adult I've had fireworks on the Fourth. Even when I was a kid I'd manage to find some firecrackers to buy so I could blow up the model airplanes I'd built over the winter. Mother didn't approve. Dad thought it was pretty cool, and probably would have joined Mickey Baylor and me in gluing Black Cats under the wings of a DC-3 or a B-24, but Mother would have had a fit. Later on, when rockets and Roman candles and cones were easier to get, I graduated to them. By the time I was seventeen I had a regular show worked out and kids would be waiting by the vacant lots at the end of our street for me to pull up in my tomato red Datsun and unload the trunk. Now it's a regular event and the one year I had pneumonia and couldn't have a show, I got get well cards from a dozen people I didn't even know. The envelopes were just addressed to "The Fireworks Guy," at my address.

The guys were looking at all the different displays and rockets. Rusty was drooling over the M-80s and Cherry Bombs. "Damn," said Rusty, "these are cheap. I wish we still had some money. How much do we have left?"

"We don't have any. I have about fifty dollars in cash and we need one more tank full of gas to get home."

"Can't we buy anything?"

I gathered the guys together and asked, "If you still had some money left, how much would you spend on this stuff?" Everybody agreed that if they each had a fifty dollar bill they could get everything they wanted. Rusty figured five hundred dollars worth of Cherry Bombs would be just about right.

I reached in my shoe and took out my credit card. "I'm going to buy everything I need for my show. You can each find fifty dollars worth and

I'll put it on my card. As long as Tangee hasn't run it up past its limit while I've been gone." That was a real worry since she'd been alone for nearly two weeks, and nothing makes time go by like shopping.

"You had a credit card?" asked Mink. I nodded.

"And we had to eat hot dogs for three solid days?" said Rusty. "We could have been eating real food and staying in motels. Why didn't you tell us?"

"I was saving it for an emergency. Now we're almost home and this is enough of an emergency for me. Now, go find some fireworks."

I went over to the center card table and talked to the man who seemed to be in charge. He looked like the kind of man whose friends would call Tiny. The folding chair he was sitting on was barely visible beneath him. A pair of four-year-olds played in the dirt off to his side.

"Hi," I said.

"Howdy."

"You've got good stuff," I said. He fanned his face with a copy of Monster Truck World and nodded.

"I'm thinking I'd probably like to buy quite a bunch. What kind of discount you think I might get?"

"I don't generally discount," he said. Then he curled his face a little and asked, "How much is a bunch?"

"Oh, maybe five hundred dollars. Maybe a thousand." My Fourth of July shows are famous.

"Hmmm," said the man. "Okay. I'll give you twenty percent on cones and displays and small rockets. Twenty five on snakes and sparklers and novelties."

"Big rockets?" I asked.

"Nope. Nothing off on big rockets. I sell out every year."

"I like big rockets," I said.

"You come here," he said and swung out of his chair. "Linda. Linda!" he called. A scrawny little woman with a hugely pregnant belly came out of the van. "You mind the store and watch the kids." She rocked over to the folding chair and lowered herself down, using both hands for balance.

"Come on," he said, and I walked behind the line of card tables and followed him to the van.

"No discount on big rockets," he repeated. "But, you're going to spend that kind of money, you might like something like this."

We stepped through the back door of the van and he pulled a tarp aside. I grinned. "You want a real show, this is what you got to have." He motioned with his arm, "Here's what they call Blue Angles. They do something with cobalt I think. You get three stages of bursts, each one a little higher in the sky and they're bright blue with some white magnesium sparkles. Here's Big Busters; a single red or green burst and a bang that'll knock your socks off. These is Cameos…you get a single report that's not as loud as a Big Buster, but then there's this huge shower of white and gold. Cameos is one of my favorites."

I looked over the Cameos and Green Spinner Dragons and the Hell Daisies as he quoted me prices on each one. "Generally I just sell these to my regulars, but if we're talking a thousand dollars I'll let you buy some."

"Five hundred to a thousand," I reminded him.

Tiny had Linda find some cardboard boxes and I started filling them. The choosing and buying part is almost as much fun as the show. It's the only thing I buy that helps me understand how women love shopping.

The other guys had picked their own selections and Linda had added up their totals. Tiny and I finished loading my boxes while she wrote a receipt and racked through my credit card. We loaded the fireworks in the bus and Tiny said, "Now you boys be careful with your smoking. Touch this stuff off and you'll be back in Michigan a whole lot faster than you'd planned on."

We headed east, comparing notes on what we'd bought. Rusty had his Cherry Bombs. Louis and Leonard Pant had bought a variety of things. Mink got mostly novelties, like a little tank that when you light the fuse it scoots forward and shoots its cannon and then goes backwards and shoots it again. He also got a bunch of sparklers and some cones. "Not much action in those things," said Rusty. "It's for the neighbor kids," said Mink. As we rode I started planning my show.

When we stopped for lunch I called Tangee from a pay phone. She wasn't home so I left a message that I'd probably be walking in the front door around seven o'clock. The closer we got to home, the more uncomfortable the bus seat was. No way I scrunched around would settle me down. I was very eager to park the bus, drive to my house and hug my wife. I started picturing what kind of welcome I would get. Most often, when I've been out of town for a few days, I find her waiting for me in the bedroom in a new negligee. Variations on this theme involve lots of candles and the bathtub. One time I turned in to the driveway around midnight and found her leaning against the maple tree, stark naked. She had a blanket on the ground and we never made it into the house. Since it would still be light when I arrived, I doubted I'd see that one this time, even though I enjoyed it very much.

The bus bumped into Mink's driveway, I felt a click, and the purple orangutan popped out of the seat gears. The seat slid back an inch and my back quit hurting. I stopped the bus for the last time. We all did a lot of hand shaking and luggage grabbing. I was in my car ten minutes later and home twenty minutes after that. I left my stuff in the car and walked in the front door.

Tangee was in the bathroom touching up her makeup. She was wearing a pair of very nice tailored gray slacks, heels and a navy blue blazer over a fluffy white turtleneck sweater. Her purse was on the counter.

"Oh, Bucky! I'm so glad your home!"

I gave her a big hug and a kiss. Generally, after the first big kiss there's a second one and then the third one when you both feel the air go out of your lungs and one of you goes, "Hmmmmfff...." I only got the one big kiss and then a much, much smaller one. She turned back to the mirror to fix her lipstick. Then she looked at her watch.

"It's okay," she said, "I still have time. Tell me all about your trip."

"Ah...why don't we sit down...or something?"

"I've only got a few minutes," she said. "I don't want to be late for work."

Blink

"Oh. I've got a job."

"How? What?" This was definitely not the naked-by-the-maple-tree welcome.

"Okay. Come sit down. Okay. See…remember that newspaper story about the two thousand year old letter from Jesus Christ and how you told me it was all a lie and how I told you I was going over to Channel Seven on Monday to see? Well, I did. I got all dressed up nice and put my hair part way up with curls on the side and I went. And you know, they hadn't even ever heard of that letter and worse than that they laughed at me." She checked her watch again. "So then I went over to Channel Four. They were nicer because they didn't laugh, but they said that kind of story wasn't really news. Then I went to channel twenty-one."

Channel twenty-one is a local independent station. They show a lot of reruns and several programs that they produce themselves about psychics and fortune tellers and people who were abducted by UFOs. They also have a news department that has promotional ads during the day saying things like, "Ground glass in your children's tofu? For a report and film you won't want to miss, see News Twenty-One at eleven." There's never really any ground glass to report, but I guess they like to warn you about things that just might could maybe happen someday.

Tangee went on, "I showed them the headline about the two thousand year old letter from Jesus Christ and they didn't laugh. In fact, some of them had seen that story already. I asked if it was true and they said that it just might be. I told them there were lots of good stories like that out there in these different newspapers and that they really ought to have somebody checking them out and reporting on them. Three people from the news department, some manager guy and a secretary told me to have a seat and they went into this other room and had a meeting. When they came out they asked if I had a job and I said no and they asked if I'd like to be Assistant Local Alternative News Reporter. They said they'd pay me and I could join the Union and everything. And so, that's why I have to go. We were going to tape this week's segment this afternoon, but Mandi Ann was out of town." Tangee had stood up and was heading out the front door. "I'll be home in about two hours."

I walked her to her car. I asked, "Mandi Ann? You mean Mandi Ann Sobosinski? You show her the stories and she actually reports on them during the news show?" Mandi Ann Sobosinski had been the weather person at channel seven until about five years ago when she left to have a baby.

"Well, yes I show them to her and then she decides how to research it and then she and some guy at the station do that and then me and Mandi Ann talk about it."

"You're on TV?"

"Uh huh. Not tonight, though. We tape once a week and it airs on Thursday afternoon and then again at eleven twenty. I love you, Bucky. I'll be home soon. Bye bye."

My wife was on TV. I left home for two weeks and my wife winds up on TV. I watched her back down the driveway. Then I unloaded my stuff from my car and unpacked in the house. I felt kind of empty. I had all these adventures to tell her and all we do is talk for fifteen minutes about her job that I didn't even know she had and she rushes off because now she's a TV star. No new negligee, either.

I watched TV for a little while and then she called from her cell phone to say she was on her way home. When she pulled in the driveway, I was waiting by the maple tree. After that we talked all night.

The next morning we slept in because I was still on vacation and had been gone for almost two weeks and Tangee and I had some catching up to do. We also talked some more. At about ten thirty I decided I'd better get started on my fireworks display since the next day was the Fourth of July.

I dragged my rocket launcher tubes and display racks out of the garage and dusted them off. Then I sorted through all my new fireworks and made an inventory. From there I drew up some notes and sketches on a yellow legal pad and checked my inventory again and made a few changes. I made a quick run to the local roadside sweet corn and fireworks stand and spent another fifty dollars for the few items I hadn't gotten before. I spent the rest of the day wiring and duct taping Roman candles and showering fountains to my plywood racks. I have a big roll of fuse I bought a few years ago, and I rig it among each of the displays so that each one will go off in the right order. I have four different racks and I filled each one. Then I skidded them back into the garage. I leave the rocket tubes until the actual show and fill them as I go. Most years Roy helps me keep them loaded as the show goes on. I get to light them, though. I had already checked the Weather Channel and it looked like light winds and only the slightest chance of showers. When I get rained out or winded out I move the show to the next weekend date. Nobody needs to be told, they just come back on the right day.

The morning of the Fourth was sweet and hot and still. By noon it was close to ninety with the sun hot on my head as I sat on my lawn chair and smoked and imagined how it would all go in about ten hours. I had to laugh at how really stupid it all was. I spent all that money and did all this planning and folks would come from all over to watch my puny little fireworks when all they had to do was look up at noon time and see the biggest firework of them all, right overhead. There's no accounting for fun, I guess.

At eight o'clock Roy came over and helped me skid my display racks and my rocket tubes over to the vacant lot across the street. I did a lot of checking to make sure that all of my fuse connections were still in place and I lined up the skyrockets in the order I wanted them shot off in. First there would be a rack display and then a bunch of rockets, then another display and then more rockets and so on. I was guessing the whole thing would take at least twenty minutes and it might go as long as three-quarters of an hour. Of course, none of it is legal. Last year we had three police cruisers and a car from the Sheriffs' office parked in the front yard. There were about a dozen cops sitting on the trunks of those black and white Crown Victorias going oooh and ahhh with the rest of the neighbors. I guess they figure it must be okay as long as I finish before eleven o'clock and they give me a warning when the show's over and they don't drink any of the beer.

People started to gather around nine. There were lawn chairs in my front yard and all around the vacant lot. Cars were parked all up and down my street. A good crowd. Roy got there about nine thirty and we rechecked all of my fuse connections. It was getting pretty dark. I said to Roy, "Okay," and we lit the first fuse, "It's showtime!

I had started with fifteen cones of different colors, all timed to go off in groups of three. They were just duct taped to a two-by-four on the ground and didn't make much of a sight but it got everybody's attention. For just a second everybody got quiet and then you could hear, "It's starting. Shh. Oh, look." I like the first few minutes when things are just getting started. In the light of the silver and blue sparks I moved over to the first rack. It was three, four-by-eight pieces of plywood fixed together, and was arranged with dozens of cones and sparklers and Roman candles. I lit the fuse and just as my first cones were going out, the rack came to life. The theme was silver and red in the shape of a heart. One after another the pieces lit and formed more of the picture: a giant silver heart made of sparklers surrounding smaller hearts of red and silver cones, all shooting off sparks at the same time. Right before the hearts were at their brightest, a series of blue displays shot through the middle of the hearts in the shape of an arrow and the letters "B & T" lit up. That one got a lot of applause and a round of, "Aws." As the first rack faded and sputtered away we lit off the first of the rockets. People love rockets. They pointed and oohed and ahhed and so did I.

We worked our way through the racks and the rockets up to the grand finale, a four by eight sheet of plywood set to shower red, white and blue sparkles in the shape of the American flag. I walked back into my yard to watch that one and let Roy set off the last of the rockets.

I stood in my yard and watched red rockets squirt up toward the moon. The sparkles were fuzzy through all the fireworks smoke. Very nice. There were a few strangers in my yard but I didn't mind; the show's for everybody.

A few feet from me was a woman I didn't recognize. "Kind of a nice show, huh?" I said. "It certainly is," she answered. I lit a cigarette.

She waved her hand. I exhaled. She waved both arms. "Do you mind!?" she said.

"Yeah, I mind," I said, "it's my yard!"

"Well, it's my air you are fouling."

I said, "Then go breathe your air in your yard."

It had been a really nice evening and I didn't want to spoil it, so I looked for someone else to talk to. Standing by my maple tree I found Leonard Pant, Rusty, Mink and Louis.

"You guys should have come over," I said. "I would have let you light some rockets off."

"That's okay," said Mink. "It was fun just to watch."

"Great show, Buck," said Rusty. Louis nodded and even Leonard Pant shook my hand.

"Hey, look," said Rusty. "Over there. Isn't that Scuddy? I haven't seen him since we got back."

Rusty waved and Scuddy waved back and started walking over to us. He was hand in hand with a girl. Scuddy didn't have a girlfriend the last time I saw him.

"Geez, Scuddy, it's good to see you," said Louis. "Too bad you couldn't come along with us. We had fun."

"I felt real bad about that," said Scuddy. "But it was my sister. You know. And besides," he put his arm around the girl, "it turned out okay."

"Yeah," said Rusty, "who's this?"

Scuddy introduced us to Melinda and she smiled.

"Yeah," Scuddy went on, "the day you guys left I was really down. I had planned on coming down to see you guys off that morning, but it kind of made me sad, so I didn't. I just stayed home all day. Then the next day I got up and said to myself, what the heck, I've still got the gas money you guys gave me back. So I went down to one of the casinos in Detroit. I know it's not the same as the places you guys probably stayed, but they're nice."

"Yeah," said Leonard Pant, "we stayed in some real classy places. Remind me to tell you sometime about the Blue Lake Camp Ground."

"I bet," said Scuddy, "but I had a pretty good time. I went down early in the afternoon and played Blackjack for about four hours."

"You must have been doing pretty good to play for four hours," I said.

"About even, mostly. The first hour was fun. Then after the next two hours it got to be routine. The last hour was more like work. My back hurt and I just kept playing one hand after the other. I'd win a few and lose a few but overall I was staying even. At one point I was almost hoping I'd bust so I could leave. Then I got up a hundred dollars and said the hell with it and quit."

"A hundred dollars isn't bad for four hours," said Louis.

"No. It was okay. I just kept thinking about how much better a time you guys were having. So anyway, on my way out I stopped at a slot machine…"

"Oh, geez," said Rusty. "You should have quit with the hundred."

"No," said Scuddy. "I won."

"Really? You won on the slots? How much?"

"Ah," Scuddy looked down, "twelve thousand dollars."

Nobody said a word.

"And then I went home," he said.

"You went home?"

"Yup. I took my sister to dinner and we rented a movie and that was it for that day."

"You won twelve thousand dollars and all you can think of is having dinner with your sister? No other celebrating? Nothing?" Rusty was amazed. "I would have been out on the town, man. I would have been…"

"We know what you would have been doing, Rusty," said Mink.

"You're damn right, I would have. And you didn't do anything, Scuddy? Really?"

"Not that day," he answered.

"Ah ha!" said Rusty.

Melinda was all snuggled up by Scuddy's side.

"Well," he started, "the next day after I mowed the lawn, I figured like what you said. So I got cleaned up and went to a bar."

"What kind of bar, Scuddy?" Rusty was interested.

"Yeah, well, a topless bar actually. I knew you guys would be out doing stuff so I figured I had some money so I'd do that stuff too."

Melinda said, "But not any more, huh?" Scuddy smiled. Melinda wandered a few yards away and sat under the maple tree.

"It was that real hot day a few weeks ago. Oh, yeah, you guys weren't here. It was hot and the air was heavy and even the sky looked funny. So I go to this topless bar and it's almost empty. I mean there are only two other guys in there and eight topless dancers. Turns out there was this tornado warning and I didn't even know it and I guess that's why there weren't more guys there. I'd planned to maybe go back to the casino after the bar so I had some cash on me. Anyway, the girls found out I had some money and the two other guys didn't and before I know it I've got about six of them sitting by me. I put a couple hundred dollars on the table and they stayed with me most of the afternoon. They kind of split up the cash among themselves."

"All afternoon?" said Rusty, still amazed.

"Yup. They gave me dances and sometimes even more than one of them was half naked and dancing right there for me."

"You got doubles?" Rusty knew the vocabulary.

"Yeah and we all had lunch and talked and they talked with each other about stuff and guys and things."

"Did they talk dirty?" asked Rusty.

"Ah, well, they were talking about their boyfriends and sex and customers. I guess I got to hear a lot of girl talk. Yeah, they were talking pretty nasty. But it was fun. It was great. Then I left."

Rusty looked like he couldn't believe anybody would ever leave. He certainly wouldn't have, but then if it had been him, maybe all of the girls wouldn't have hung around so much. Scuddy is a really nice guy. Rusty is Rusty.

"Then I went back to the casino. I still had a few hundred dollars in my pocket and thought I might get lucky again." Melinda walked back to us. Scuddy went on, "I met her," and he smiled.

"At the casino?" said Rusty. "You met her there?"

"Yup. At the slot right next to where I'd won the twelve thousand. I put a few dollars into the machine, but I didn't win. She went broke the same time I did. We started talking. We had a drink and talked some more. Then we went to Mexican Town for enchiladas and just kept on talking. The next night we went out and the night after that, too. We went to a concert. Neil Diamond."

"A Neil Diamond impersonator?" asked Rusty.

"No. The real guy. It was a great show. And you know that singer, Dianna Ross? Well, some friend of hers from high school or something was getting married and she was in town for the wedding and went to the show and she got up on stage and sang a song with Neil Diamond. And, yeah, it was the real Dianna Ross."

"Neil Diamond, Dianna Ross, and you won twelve thousand dollars and had a whole topless club to yourself and on top of everything you met her?"

"Yup. But I'm still sorry I missed the trip with you guys." Melinda whispered something to Scuddy and he smiled again. "We got to go. Great show, Buck. I'm glad you guys had a good time. See you at poker next week?" We all nodded as they turned and walked down my driveway, outlined in the last of my fireworks. Melinda turned back to wave.

"You know the damnedest thing?" said Rusty, still gazing at Melinda's silhouette. "Her ribcage…it's perfect."

Chapter 3
Things that Happened

The Fourth of July turned into the fifth of July and I spent the day cleaning up burned out fireworks from the vacant lot. The day was hot with a misty rain that felt more like steam. The sky was the color of automobile primer paint. The cardboard rocket tubes were soggy and the half-full trash bag weighed a ton. By the time I was done I had eight bags. I dragged them to the side of the road and hoped that the trash people wouldn't mind that they were so heavy. They are picky about what they pick up and sometimes just leave things lying there. I rolled our regular trash to the road jammed into two barrels. I usually use three barrels but one of them was pretty old and the bottom was almost out of it, so I took that one to the road and stomped it flat and laid it on top of the other barrels. The next morning the fireworks bags were gone and the regular trash was gone and my two barrels were lined up on their sides. The stomped on barrel lay next to them. I dragged all three back to the garage wondering to myself how I'd ever be able to get rid of the busted can. How do you throw out a trash can? I had a week to think about it.

If the Fourth of July is my holiday, the rest of the year belongs to

Tangee. Her home-decorating year starts with Valentine's Day. I have to drag out the pink and white six-foot tall plywood heart with the pink and white lights hung on it and she changes the clothes on the concrete goose so that he looks like a little cupid. For Memorial Day we do lots of flags and red, white and blue lights and they stay up for the Fourth of July and Labor Day. The pink flamingoes on the lawn get little Uncle Sam hats.

By the first of October Tangee's decorating juices get going again and she starts planning our Halloween display. Along with the red-lit graves and plastic tombstones we've got about a thousand feet of orange Christmas style lights and my stereo speakers buried in the lawn playing spooky sounds. If there isn't any wind we hang a bucket of water from the tree and drop dry ice in as the night goes along. I point my old eight-millimeter movie projector at the dry ice fog and show a movie of ghosty shapes. The flamingos get teeny, tiny vampire teeth and black capes. If we do too much it scares away the little kids and we wind up with a bunch of left over candy corn and milk duds. Sometimes I get bad dreams about the flamingoes.

But Halloween is just a warm-up. Christmas is the main event.

It was early December and Tangee was studying our plaster lawn population, "No," she said, "it's the fairies, then the elves, then the gnomes."

I said, "But last year it was the other way—gnomes first."

"No, I remember, it goes by size, tallest to smallest."

"Oh, okay, I'm sorry. I thought it was fattest to skinniest." I reset their little plaster feet in the dead grass.

"That's better. See? Now it's just like a little parade and they're all on they're way to see the baby Jesus."

"Looks like they're on their way to see Santa Claus, too," I said. "Should he really be so close to the manger?"

"Oh, you're just like those people on the contest committee. Maybe we shouldn't have had Santa sitting on the roof of the manger last year, but we still should have won."

The Huron Bay Beacon runs a contest every year for the best decorated home, and every year somebody else wins.

Tangee said, "I still think the Ozinskis paid off somebody at the newspaper. All they had were plain white and blue lights and some kind of tinsel stuff blowing in the wind. I bet that was a mess to clean up. We had twice as many lights as they did and all colors too, not just white and blue. And we had a manger and the gnomes and we had a Santa."

"And Santa on the roof of the stable," I reminded her.

"It was only silly because stables don't have chimneys. We should have thought of that. This year he's just standing there."

"Yup," I said, "the fourth wise man."

"Too close?" she asked.

"Yeah, I think so."

Tangee looked up at the roof of the house and said, "I just wonder where we could put him, then?"

"Oh, no," I said. "Oh, no. I told you, nothing on the roof. Period."

"But, Buck, it's mild and nice and there's no snow yet and you could just tie the big inflatable Santa to the chimney with a bungee cord and maybe string a few hundred lights around the eaves. We wouldn't have to use the reindeer."

"Nope. It's nice now, but in January you're going to want him down and it's not going to be so nice then, and there's going to be ice and I'm not going to do it."

"Maybe you wouldn't have to take him down."

I shook my head. "You're the one who gets depressed when you see people with their Christmas stuff up halfway into spring. You're the one who drives two blocks out of her way so you won't have to see the wreath Gwen and Phyllis leave up until June. You're the one who called the police to see if there was a law about leaving wreaths up out of season."

"Well, then," she said, "long about the second week of January, if it was icy, maybe you could just go out in the yard with your twenty-two and deflate him." Tangee must have caught a mental picture of a shot, deflated, plastic Santa hanging from a bunge cord from the chimney until April. She shook her head, dismissing the idea.

"Well, what are we going to do then?" she said. "We have to have something special with the Santa Claus. We've got the gnomes and all and we got the manger and we got lights around all the windows and in all the shrubs and on the mailbox. We got the spinning aluminum tree by the garage. It's all very classy but I think we need something splashy to win the contest. I just don't know."

Tangee looked sad and defeated as she walked out to the street to view what we'd done so far. Just before the ditch we've got what's left of a hedge running parallel to the road. It had grown to about two feet high before that problem with the sewer killed it. She walked past the dead hedge and past the ditch and across the street to get a judge's eye view of the yard. She came back grinning.

"Is the ground froze?" she asked.

"No, I don't think so."

"Have we still got those iron clothes poles in the garage?"

"Yup. Up in the rafters. Why?"

"Bucky, this will be perfect. When the judges drive by and stop in front of our house, they'll see all of our decorations, just like we've got them, but they'll see them through a kind of picture frame." She brought me into the house to explain.

The idea was that we'd trim the dead hedge bushes to look like mountains and spray them with phony snow and cover them with forty strings of white blinking lights. Then we'd string a wire between the two metal clothes poles, which I would have pounded in the ground. The last thing would be that we'd hang the inflatable Santa in his sled along with his eight inflatable reindeer from the wire. The judges would look through the scene of Santa flying over the mountains to view the gnomes and the manger and the aluminum tree.

The next day was a Sunday. I made Tangee promise that if I got all of that work done by Saturday night, she'd let me watch football and nap the next day. I'll do some awful things to get a guaranteed football/nap day. I was done by midnight.

Judging was the second Saturday of December and Tangee was beside herself waiting for the big day. She kept busy by planting a forest of candy canes in front of Fat Boy's doghouse and making other important finishing touches. The pink flamingoes got halos and angel wings. We turned on the hedge lights one time to make sure they worked…Tangee was worried about showing the total effect too early in case somebody wanted to steal her idea.

The Friday night before the judging she couldn't sleep and went outside at midnight with flashlight and a jar of blue craft paint to retouch the baby Jesus' eyes. At four in the morning she plugged in all the lights for a minute to make sure they'd work. From six AM until noon she watched the Weather Channel, worrying about a frontal system in Wisconsin which might or might not make it to our house before the committee drove by at seven-thirty. She made a walk around the yard at one in the afternoon and came back in a panic.

"It's Dasher and Dancer," she wailed. "They're deflating. You have to do something."

I dragged the ladder out to the display and found she was right; the lead pair of deer were shriveling and Dancer's head was half folded over. Dasher's air filler cap was located just about where I expect you'd find a reindeer's navel. I prayed nobody I knew would drive by while I was reinflating. It didn't matter. The more I inflated the more Dasher deflated. There was a leak. In fact, just at the base of Dancer's neck a whole seam was coming apart.

"Bucky, what are we going to do? Look. Comet and Cupid are leaking, too."

"Maybe we could fill them with something," I suggested.

"Like newspapers?" she asked.

"Maybe. Or, we still have a whole bunch of that Styrofoam popcorn-shaped packing stuff don't we? I could make a hole and fill them with that and seal it with duct tape."

"Anything, Bucky. Hurry."

It worked. Dasher and Dancer filled out just fine, and to make sure the other deer and Santa Claus didn't have the same problem, I filled them with Styrofoam, too. They were a little lumpy but I didn't figure you could tell that from the road.

By six o'clock it was dark. At seven we turned on the hedge

lights. A half-hour later we saw three cars full of judges, driving slowly up the street, pausing at each display.

Santa floated gently over the hedge mountains with the phony snow and the four thousand blinking white lights and the thick billows of drifting clouds. Exactly as planned. Except for the clouds. We hadn't planned on thick puffy white clouds drifting over the hedge. We also hadn't planned on a fire in the hedge, which was where the puffy smoke was coming from. One of the forty strands of lights must have shorted out.

The puffy white clouds turned black as the phony snow caught fire. Two by two the reindeer smoldered into brown lumps hanging over the flames. Then the judges stopped. They watched for what seemed to be a very long time. I stood in the doorway next to Tangee. She was crying. The judges left just before the fire department got there. I helped clean up and Tangee went to bed early.

It was real quiet at our house the next morning. The paper came at noon. We were front-page news. I read the story to Tangee.

"Congratulations to Buck and Tangee Crimmins on winning the annual Christmas décor contest! Although there were many beautiful displays this year, the committee decided that the Crimmins' originality should be rewarded. Their spectacular interpretation of 'The Christmas Song' is well worth our first prize."

I held up the accompanying picture, showing the brown plastic lumps hanging just above the licking flames of the hedge.

"The Christmas Song?" Tangee asked.

"Sure. Remember? 'Chestnuts roasting on an open fire?'"

She put the prize, a golden wreath, on the mantle. Next year I think we'll stick to gnomes and the spinning aluminum tree.

Usually we leave Christmas decorations up for the two weeks following the holiday, but Tangee was so proud of her award that they stayed up until the end of January. She helped me take everything down and then I drove over to get some gas in my pickup.

*

I ran into my friend, Marty, at the Amoco station. He was pumping regular and I was pumping mid-grade. He had his back to a puffy

August wind and it had blown the back of his hair into a rooster tail. "Hey, Buck," he said, "how does it feel to be famous?"

"Me? I'm not famous for anything, Marty. What are you talking about?"

"Don't you know? You're in a book…in a story. You and Tangee."

I couldn't imagine why me and my wife would be in anybody's book or story or anything unless maybe it was the world record book. Maybe they finally got her letter and let us in for having the world's longest continuous string of Christmas lights.

"I was in the dentist's office," said Marty, hanging up the filler hose, "and while I was waiting I was reading this magazine called American Literary Short Fiction Review. Really. I was that bored. It's all they had." He sounded defensive. "There was a story in it about you guys. About the time you took Tangee and her uncle fishing."

"Really?" I said.

"Yeah, and you know what? I think it was written by Willy Zink. Except his name was maybe spelled different. And he didn't call you by your right names. He called you Butch and Maybelline, but it was you guys all right."

I went right from the Amoco station to the library and then to the Shade Tree BookStore, but neither of them had ever heard of the American Literary Short Fiction Review, so I went to Marty's dentist's office. I traded them three fairly recent copies of Field and Stream for the Review and took it home. I read the story by William Scinque called, "Fishing Trip: A Butch and Maybelline Story."

It sure enough was about the time that I took Tangee and her uncle, Benny, fishing with me. The story was almost pretty funny, but there were parts in it that weren't at all how I remembered the trip. Like, I don't recall seeing Tangee floating down the stream with her sundress all puffed up around her like a balloon and looking like Ophelia from the play Hamlet. The puffed up balloon part was right, but I'd never in my life thought about Tangee being connected with anything from Shakespeare. I thought she looked like a jellyfish, and that's what I told her as she floated away. That's why she tried to reach out and swat me and that's why the air leaked out of her sundress balloon and she started to sink and I had to throw her Benny's hemorrhoid cushion tied to a fishing line so I could pull her in. That was what really happened and I thought it was a whole lot funnier the way it turned out than what Willie said about Ophelia. I guess Ophelia is more literary.

I found Willie at the Do-Nut Shoppe. I know him from The Beer Bar and the Lakeshore Autoparts Plaza and the Do-Nut Shoppe. Willie's a quiet little guy and he works in an office for some computer company. At the Beer Bar he doesn't talk much, but he's a good listener and he laughs at the right places when you tell a joke.

"Hey, Bucky, how you doing?" he asked. He fumbled in his pocket and came out with a cigarette and a Bic lighter.

"I'm okay," I said. I plopped the magazine on the counter, jingling his silverware and blowing crumbs onto his lap. "What's with this?" I asked.

"Boy, that didn't take long," said Willie, swallowing hard and putting down his coffee cup. "Want a doughnut?"

"Yeah. A sour cream one. And a coffee, too." I was trying to sound mean. "So?"

Willie reached back in his shirt pocket and took out a little recorder. It was running. He turned it off.

"You tell some funny stories." I had to give him credit for looking me square in the eye. "People laugh. Did you know I write stories?"

"Nope."

"Ever since I was a kid," said Willie. "I've written mystery stories and romance stories and just anything I could think of. I've got hundreds of them. I send them to magazines, but I never got one published."

"So what?" I said.

"So, you always have all this funny stuff happening to you. Or, at least the way you tell it is funny. So I did this," and he nudged the little recorder.

"You taped me?"

"Yeah. And I wrote down about the fishing story and I fixed it up a little bit and sent it in and they published it."

"You fixed it up a little? You fixed up my life? I thought you said it was funny already."

"It is, but they like to have lots of other stuff in stories. You have to write about how the clouds look and the way the grass feels and you have to come up with all these other things."

"Like how Tangee looked like Ophelia?"

"Just like that."

"So now what's going to happen?" I asked.

"What do you mean?"

"I mean I have to decide if I'm going to bust you in the head or sue you for writing about us without permission or what."

"I guess you have to hit me, then, because you can't sue me…I got a right to write about whatever I want to. I changed your names and I changed enough other things so that I can say you're fictional."

I didn't like the idea of being fictional. I didn't like the idea of somebody else writing about me and Tangee. If anybody was going to do any writing about us, it was going to be me. I left Willie to worry about what I might do and drove home.

The next day was slow at work and I was going to go home at noon. I put away the papers on my desk and made a few notes on my yellow legal pad of things I had to do tomorrow. I tore off the page and taped it to the coffee maker. Then I looked at the blank writing pad. Then I started to write.

I wrote about the day Tangee and I went to the Festival of Renaissance Art and Life, where there are people all made up like they were living in the Middle Ages and there are jousts and jesters and everything. A lot of funny stuff happened that day and I figured if Willie could get a story published about our fishing trip, I could do the same about the Festival.

When I stopped writing it was dark outside and I'd run out of legal paper and had finished up on the back of an old calendar and last month's phone bill. I read what I'd written and it still seemed funny to me, so I folded up the papers and the phone bill and February through June and put them in a file. Then I drove home.

Tangee can be a real good cook when she sets her mind to it.

When I walked into the house I knew it was spaghetti night, which I like a lot. We fixed our plates and went out to the TV room so we could watch the old reruns of Friends while we ate. I told her about us being in a story by Willie Zink and she got mad and thought he should have paid us for our story. I told her I didn't much care about him getting the money, but that I thought I could do a better job of telling it than him.

"Do you remember the Festival of Renaissance Art and Life we went to two years ago?" I asked.

She nodded, picking mushrooms out of the sauce.

"Today at work, I wrote down how that day went. I'm going to send it to that magazine so they can print stuff about us the way it really happened, not the way Willie would write it."

"Would somebody really pay you for a story just about us going to that fair?"

"They paid Willie," I said.

"That was a fun day, huh?" said Tangee with a little smile. Then she lost the smile. "You didn't write about when I bought that pheasant (sic) blouse, did you?"

"Yup," I said around a mouthful of salad.

"You can't put that in!"

We'd seen ads for the Festival of Renaissance Art and Life on TV for a few weeks. There were video shots of knights on horses and ladies in flowing dresses and pointy hats with ribbons on them and jesters with bells on their hats and shoes. The announcer said in a very British accent, "Come! Come to the Shire of Ardmore! Live a life gone these five hundred years! Dine with the King and Queen! Joust with the Black Knight!" It sounded pretty cool.

It was a sweet October afternoon. Lots of high fast clouds blew overhead but there wasn't much wind on the ground. The Festival covered about forty acres outside the little town of Ardmore. There were thirty acres of cars. We had to park on the road and walk a mile and a half. Lines of people funneled through the gates, dropping twelve dollars and fifty cents each at Ye Olde Ticket Booth. Inside the gates a road of foot-packed dirt forked right and left, lined with shops designed to look old. We turned right and stopped at the first food booth we came to and got some New World Lemon-aide for three dollars a cup. Slices of squashed lemon floated in the crushed ice. We strolled from shop to shop.

"Does everybody who's got a costume on work here?" asked Tangee.

I said, "No, I think lots of people who paid to get in are dressed up too."

"You should have worn one of those," said Tangee pointing to a guy wearing tights and a short jacket.

"I don't think I'd make a very good Robin Hood, but I might do it if you'd dress like that," and I nodded toward a woman in a long velvet dress with a deep, deep scoop for a neckline.

"She's almost falling out of that," said Tangee. "I couldn't ever…"

"Well then I'm not going to wear any Robin Hood tights. My big old butt would stick out."

I followed Tangee's eyes as Robin approached and realized his butt wasn't the only thing emphasized by his outfit. Tangee blushed.

Over the next hour we looked at probably a hundred booths. About half of them sold candles or jewelry or gnomes carved out of wood.

"Now, that's cute," said Tangee as a girl walked by wearing a simple skirt and a loosely cut peasant blouse. We'd seen a few places selling clothes but we hadn't actually shopped in any of them. We were almost back to the entrance gate when we found one more. It was Mistress Elysia's Seamstress Shoppe. We went in.

Mostly, when Tangee goes shopping for clothes, I stay home. Or if it's in a mall I sit on a bench by the indoor trees and read a book. I just hate standing outside the changing room at Chix holding on to three different sizes of pants, a couple of tops and various bras and slips while Tangee pops in and out of the room to model and ask if something fits right or not. As if I'd know the right answer. I know that nobody thinks I'm waiting for a room to try the stuff on myself, but it's still uncomfortable. I didn't feel quite so stupid at Mistress

Elysia's. There were other guys there waiting for their wives or girlfriends and besides, Mistress Elysia sold some men's wear too. I held up a green Robin Hood jacket.

"That's a jerkin," said Mistress Elysia. "Very popular. I think you'd take an extra large." She found one and held it up to my shoulders. "And you'd wear it with these," she went on, holding up a coat hanger from which a pair of tights dangled, all shriveled looking like a sad, sagging balloon.

"Not exactly my style," I said. Outside the wooden walls of the Shire of Ardmore a man would have to have an ego a whole lot bigger than mine to wear a thing like that in public. Even inside the walls it took some guts. In addition to the tights, there was a curved foam thing dangling from the hanger by a string. It was concave and shaped like a big comma.

"That's the codpiece," she said. "You know. For down there," and she glanced at my crotch.

"Oh, I don't think..." I started.

"Oh, yes," she said. "Really quite necessary. Otherwise, everything shows. Unless you want to show..."

I must have been blushing. She said, "It also keeps you warm. And some guys like them because it makes them look...bigger."

"A male falsie?" I asked.

She nodded.

So when Tangee finally finished plowing through the racks of blouses there I was, holding a jerkin, a deflated pair of tights and a codpiece. I told her what the codpiece was for and she laughed. She had an armload of peasant blouses and she gave me all but one to hold, "Here," she said, "hang on to these while I try this on."

The changing room was a small area set off from the rows of clothes and counters of jewelry by sheets hung from ropes and poles. She ducked in through an opening and five minutes later stuck her head out holding the blouse towards me, "Too big. Give me the next one."

The wind had picked up some and it was feeling warmer when, a few minutes later she said, "Let me try the tan one." I handed it to her and set the others down as I wandered a few feet away to study some pointy boots with bells on them. I glanced up as the wind opened a patch of blue across the sun, scooting the clouds aside. The sun felt like it was shining right through my skin. I looked over and found that the only thing the sunlight was really shining through was the white sheet wall of the changing room, with Tangee's shadow outlined right in the middle of it.

I called, "Tangee!" but she didn't hear me. I started toward the changing room but a skinny little guy in a jester suit holding a big, empty picture frame cut me off. He held the frame in front of the backlit sheet wall with one hand. In the other he had a crude sign that read, "Ye Olde Peep Show-25 Cents." Tangee's silhouette was stark against the sheet as she pulled a blouse off over her head. She reached for the next one to try on and had paused to scratch her left breast just as I got to the sheet.

I pushed the jingling twerp out of my way and slipped through the sheet corner opening. "Bucky!" she yelled. I stepped between her and the sheet, hugged her to me and whispered, "They can see." She looked puzzled for a second and then shrieked, grabbed her purse, pulled on her tee shirt and dashed with me through the back of the changing room. Lots of people were laughing. We ran until we got to a small bench under a tree about two hundred feet from Mistress Elysia's. She was crying. I hugged her and told her how we'd never see any of these people ever again and that it was just a shadow and nobody could really see all that much, all good husbandly lies.

"We're gonna sue," she sniffled as we walked to the exit gate. "We're gonna get our money back."

"You want to explain to a whole bunch of people what happened? We'd have to go back to Mistress Elysia's and show what happened. You'd have to stand behind that sheet again, but if you want to talk to the owners or managers of this place we can."

"No. I guess I just want to go home."

We were about to step out when she stopped.

"Bucky?"

"Hmmm?"

"I really liked that blouse."

"I bet it was cute on you."

"The small size fit me good. Would you buy it for me?"

"You want to go back and get it? After we ran away and everything?"

"It was a size small. In that tan color. I left it hanging in the changing room. I could wait here. It was really cute on me. Would you?"

I went back. I found the blouse. I didn't look at Mistress Elysia or anybody. The joker was gone. I gave the girl a hundred-dollar bill and didn't even count the change.

Later that night I was watching Sport Center. Tangee called from the other room, "Want to see my blouse?"

"Sure."

She stepped out of the shadow of the unlit hall and walked square in front of the TV. She was wearing the blouse, and nothing else. "Was this how I looked?" she asked. The bright picture tube flashed through the fabric, outlining her shape. I smiled and held out my arms.

And that was pretty much how the day went. I wrote it up as a story, but I didn't put in all of the conversations and description like it's printed here. That came later. Tangee wasn't very happy that I had the part in about the peasant blouse, but then I don't think she really believed that anybody would want to read about it anyway. The Review would only take submissions sent through the mail, so the next morning I typed up what I had written on my old Selectric and mailed it in to the American Literary Short Fiction Review. Then I forgot about it.

About three months later I came home from work and Tangee was practically bouncing off the walls.

"Your check is here!" she shouted before I even had my jacket off. "Open it! Open it! How much did they give you?"

The envelope from the American Literary Short Fiction Review was very impressive. Their name was embossed in blue and the seal was shiny gold.

"Open it!"

I opened it. Inside was the first page of my story. Clipped to it was a five-inch by seven-inch slip that said,

"Dear contributor;

We have read your story. Thank you for sending it to us, but the material is not suitable for our publication.

Sincerely,

Sylvia Adams-Musinski, Editor"

It was a form letter, but below in scrawled red ink was handwritten, "It is customary for contributors to enclose a stamped self-addressed envelope with submissions."

"How much?" said Tangee. "Is there a check?"

"They didn't like it, I guess," I answered quietly. I had written the story in a day and forgotten about it for twelve weeks. I was surprised at how disappointed I was, and how embarrassed I felt that I hadn't even known to send along a stamped envelope. I threw the papers away. I ate dinner and watched a Bogart film festival until I fell asleep in my TV chair at two in the morning.

Two days later I was still bummed out so I took my photo copy of the story and went to find Willie Zink. He wasn't at the Beer Bar or the Do-Nut Shoppe so I went to his office. He flinched when he saw me.

"It's okay, Willie. I'm not mad any more, but I've got to ask you about this. How come they printed your story about me but didn't like my story about me? Would you read this?"

It was almost lunchtime and we walked over the sub sandwich shop. He read while he ate. I'd been in that shop lots of times but I never noticed how the rungs in the back of the chairs dug at my spine. I watched his eyes as he read. I picked up little fallen bits of lettuce from my tray and nibbled. I tried to watch traffic.

Finally he said, "This is funny," tapping the pages. "I remember when you told us about all this at the Beer Bar. It was a better story then. You're a better story teller than you are a story writer."

"Oh."

"Now wait. Don't get me wrong. This is good. You put everything in order and you told just how it happened, but it just doesn't…I don't know…read right. Like you don't have any dialog."

I looked up from my tray.

"Conversation. What people say. When you told the story at the bar, you made your voice higher and told us how Tangee screamed and what she said and what you said back to her. That's dialog. And in the bar, I remember you putting in a lot of detail. I bet it took you twenty minutes to tell that story. I wouldn't take three minutes to read what you wrote. You left the good parts out."

"So I should have made it longer?" I asked.

"Well, it's more than that. You ever think about taking a class at the community college? Creative writing? They offer it at night and it's not just twenty-year-olds."

I checked it out and registered for a six week, twice a week class in the evening. The first night I parked in the lot and walked up to the Elmore Burlington Center of Communication Arts with a new spiral notebook in my hand and a pencil and two pens in my shirt pocket. I kept tapping my pocket with my hand to make sure the pens were still there. I checked my registration slip three times to make sure I wasn't late or early or there on the wrong day. I wondered if maybe I should have worn slacks instead of jeans. I worried about going to the wrong room and not finding out until halfway through that I was in Studies in French Literature 590 instead of Creative Writing 101. I don't know any French. I almost turned around and went home, but I didn't.

I found the room and it had a sign taped to the door that said, "Creative Writing 101, Yes This Is The Right Room." Everybody was wearing jeans, I was just on time and my pens hadn't disappeared. I sat near the back of the room, worried that I'd be called on and I wouldn't have the assignment done, even though this was the first day and there hadn't even been any assignments yet.

The first night went pretty well. The teacher was a young guy, about twenty-four, who had on jeans and a blue shirt and wore a close trimmed beard. His name was Josh and he didn't look like any of my old high school English teachers. I only got called on once and that was to tell my name and if I'd ever done any writing before. I said no. Most everybody else said yes although most of their experience was in poetry and short stories about vampires. Some had written poems about vampires. Our homework was to write a story of between five hundred and a thousand words on any subject we wanted. I would rather that he'd given us something to write about.

For the next four days I thought about nothing else but what to write about. The story about the Renaissance Fair was too long, and there wasn't anything else I thought would make a good enough story.

On Tuesday I finished up at work at five. I'd told Tangee not to expect me for dinner; I'd grab a burger on the way to class. I sat in front of the Selectric and just stared at the paper. By six I hadn't typed a single word. Then I thought, what the hell, how bad can it be, no matter what I write, compared to the other Creative Writing 101 students.

I'd always like stories about guys and their dogs so that's what I wrote. The story took place somewhere way up in Canada and there was this one guy and his dog and they're snowed in, in this cabin. In the end the guy dies. I hadn't wanted him to die but he did. It's just the way the story came out. I counted the words and they came to a little over eight hundred. I folded the paper and zipped over to the college, stopping at a drive-through for a Quarter Pounder, which I ate on the way. I was just in time. We handed in our papers and then listened to Josh talk for an hour about character, plot and setting. Our homework was to write a story that had a lot of dialog in it.

I tried to write dialog stories but they all sounded stupid. Then I remembered what Willie Zink had done, so I bought myself a little, pocket-sized, voice-activated recorder.

That Sunday afternoon Tangee was busy repotting flowers and asked me to hop over to the gift shop and buy her a blue candle. I recorded what happened and after I put in all the he saids and she saids and filled in a little, it turned out like this.

* * *

THE BLUE CANDLE
By Buck Crimmins

Tangee said, "We need a blue candle for the table."

I bought a blue candle. I *thought* I bought a blue candle.

"That's teal," she said.

"Teal's blue," I thought out loud.

"Teal's teal," she answered, "but if it's anything, it's a shade of green. Go get a blue candle. Blue."

I went. I exchanged. I came home.

"That's peacock," she said.

"Peacock's blue," I ventured. "Isn't it? I mean it's not green. Not teal. Totally blue. Right?"

She sighed, "Yes, it's blue…a shade of blue. Here, this is blue," she pointed at a pair of shoes in the Sears catalog. She was getting exasperated. "Would you rather re-pot these begonias or get a blue candle. I can't do both."

I went.

If I sent my buddy, Louis, to get something, he'd know what color I wanted. I'd say, "Ninety-two Chrysler medium metallic blue." Or, "Craftsman toolbox red." He'd know. Women don't have real life words like that. They have teal and taupe. What's a teal?

I walked back into Gwendolyn's Gifts holding the candle up to show I was back for another exchange. She nodded.

"Please," I said, "I just need a blue candle. For my wife."

She led me back to the candle aisle and picked one out, "Here you go. One blue candle."

It didn't look like the Sears shoes so I picked a different one.

Tangee looked at it when I got home and put down her potting stuff. "I'll go," she said.

"Not blue?"

"Cornflower. How can you not know what blue is? You really thought this was blue?"

"Not really," I said. "I just figured I was going to be wrong again so I picked one I liked. Same color as your eyes. Might not be blue,"

I said, "but I love it."

We kept the candle.

* * *

We turned in our stories and Josh talked for the hour about how to describe places and weather and how rooms look. I understood what he was saying but it got kind of boring. For our homework we were to write about a place. We were also assigned to go to the bookstore and buy a copy of, "Angst and Delight; Collected Short Stories."

The book was seventy pages long and was bound with a spiral of plastic. The complete title was, "Angst and Delight; Collected Short Stories by Josh Wimicki." Our teacher. It cost twenty-seven dollars. Mostly the stories were crap. I felt better about my writing, even though I only got a B+ on my candle story.

By the time the class was finished, I had written a few stories and wound up with a grade of B. That was at least two grades higher than I ever got in high school English class, but the big thing was that I found that I liked writing. I even went back and rewrote the story about the Renaissance Festival, and that's the way I put it in this book.

Six months after getting back from Las Vegas I was still getting used to the idea that Tangee had a real job. I didn't mind so much that I had to do most of the laundry, as long as I didn't have to iron. I wasn't too fond of vacuuming so I was pretty careful not to drop stuff. I kind of liked cooking.

It was Friday evening and I was making dinner. The steam from the browning pound of hamburger felt nice on my face. I drained off the grease, dumped a can of chicken gumbo soup into the pan and mixed the whole thing up to heat. I buttered a couple of pieces of toast and cut them up into little squares. Then I poured some of the chicken gumbo beef stuff on the toast and took the plate to the TV room. It's good for a man to know how to cook, especially when his wife is a TV star and gets home from work a lot later than he does.

I tuned in just in time to see Elliot Schurmer give the local weather forecast that gave a sixty percent change for snow showers in the morning. I wondered if that meant that out of a hundred days like tomorrow, it would snow on sixty of them, or if it meant that sixty percent of the metro area would get covered. I thought I ought to have Tangee ask him about that. Over a graphic of a spinning globe the announcer said, "After these messages, our own Tangee Crimmins investigates…are aliens from another galaxy infiltrating our schools?"

After the ads, news anchor Hendrick Martin filled the screen and introduced Tangee and her co-alternative news correspondent, Mandi Anne Sobosinski. Over Tangee's left shoulder was a picture of the front page of the International Investigator news tabloid and its headline, "Have Aliens taken Control of our Schools?!" Over her right shoulder floated a picture of a smooth, green extra-terrestrial with black almond shaped eyes. Over his head was a question mark.

Tangee and Mandi Anne made quite a pair with Mandi Anne having short, straight blonde hair and Tangee with hers, shoulder length, wavy and almost black. Tangee looked good. Tangee always looks good, but lately, on television, she looked even better. They say the TV camera adds a few pounds to a person's appearance, but in Tangee's case, that wasn't all bad since those pounds seemed to have been added to her boobs. She was wearing a snug red turtleneck and a necklace with a heavy pendant that rested on her chest, pressing the fabric down a little and showing shadows and contours.

It turned out that their in-depth investigations proved that the aliens in question were people from Mexico who were now the majority in several school districts. They did, however leave open the *possibility* that visitors from another planet would find it in their best interests to infiltrate school boards and influence the textbooks used by the kids.

The station went to commercial and I took my plate to the kitchen thinking happy, horny thoughts about the way that snug red turtleneck looked. The phone rang.

"Hi Bucky, it's me, what were you doing?"

"I just put my dinner dishes in the sink. Your show was good. You looked good."

"I just called to remind you that this is Friday. I'll be late. Remember to scrape your plate before you put it in the dishwasher."

"You're going out?"

"It's Friday. You know. We always go out every other week on payday. I won't be too late. Camay's coming over in the morning so we can work on those little plaster Valentines. You go ahead and eat, I'll get something at Cavern's."

"I already ate. Remember? So what time…?"

"I got to go. Everybody's waiting for me. Don't wait up. Bye. Love ya. Bye."

Tangee had told me some while ago that lots of the TV station people were involved in a Bi-Weekly Post Production Planning Meeting. It took place every other week. On payday. At a bar. Actually at Cavern's restaurant, a semi-classy place where you waited for your table in a little side lounge. I didn't mind. I figured it was good that she was getting out and making contacts with the folks she worked with. I also didn't mind because it gave me a little time to myself in the evening so I could do some writing.

Ever since I finished my writing class I'd been making notes on the things that happened on the Vegas trip. I also had lots of notes on how Roy and I had tried to make a ton of money with our BaitKing project. I planned on making them into a bunch of little stories and maybe printing them all up and putting them in a binder so I could look back on them someday.

I had converted our spare room from a storage room and Christmas present wrapping room into an office. It wasn't much of an office. Just a cheap, screw-it-together yourself desk and a chair and a filing system made our of cardboard egg crates from the supermarket. The egg crates were hard to come by because they're so good for packing and moving stuff. You have to put in your request at the grocery store on Monday to get boxes on Saturday. I also had my computer.

I had just finished printing my first pages of notes when Tangee came home. It was nearly midnight. She had strawberry Daiquiri on her breath and a little paper umbrella in her hair.

"Long meeting, huh?" I said.

"Mmm…" she answered. We stood in the middle of the living room and kissed. While we were kissing I noticed that her lips felt kind of distant so I peeked. Her eyes were open and she was looking around the room.

"Something wrong?" I asked.

"No," she said stepping back and scanning the upper corners of the walls. "It's just that I never really noticed the color of the room before."

From nowhere I remembered something and said, "It's Light Buckskin. I remember from when we picked it out and how you weren't sure if you'd like the walls to be the color of some dead animal."

"It's beige," she said. She sounded very definite and a little strange. Maybe she'd had one too many slurps of strawberry daiquiri. "It is absolutely beige. Bucky?"

"What?"

"How can we possibly live in a beige room?" She looked at the walls a bit more and toed the carpet. Then she turned and went to bed. When I followed a short while later, she was already asleep.

I got up for work the next morning to the sound of clattering dishes. I walked into the kitchen and found Tangee and Camay emptying the dishwasher. I took one of the newly cleaned cups over to the coffee maker and poured a cup. Then I held the refrigerator door open with one hand while I sipped coffee with the other.

"Do we have any liver sausage left?" I asked. "I think I'd like to take a liver sausage and cheese sandwich to work. I've been going out too much. That fast food is bad for you."

"No," said Tangee. "I threw out the last of that stuff yesterday. It was smelling bad."

"That's what liver sausage does," I said.

Camay asked, "How come you're going to work today? It's a holiday."

"I'm going to work so we can have some money so I can buy some more liver sausage. What holiday?"

"It's Ground Dog Day, Bucky. You don't have to work."

"Ground Hog Day isn't a real holiday," I said, emphasizing the word "hog."

"Of course it is," Camay went on, "it's been all over the TV. You know…the Ground Dog comes out and if he sees his snout, it's going to snow."

Tangee looked at Camay with one eyebrow lifted and said, "No Camay, it's if he sees your shadow, it's good luck. But I'm not sure if it's the kind of holiday where they don't deliver mail."

I said, "First, it's Ground *Hog* Day, not Ground *Dog* Day. Second, it's not any kind of holiday except maybe for the ground hog. And third, I don't deliver mail, I'm in construction, and if I want to go to work on Armageddon Eve I'll go."

Tangee was giving me an evil look so I grabbed my coat. "I'll just get a cheese burger," I said. I kissed Tangee and waved to Camay and walked out to my car. I couldn't figure why Camay's silliness had gotten under my skin, but it had.

Work went pretty well, but my mind kept thinking about Ground Dog Day. While I ate my double cheeseburger at lunch I decided there wasn't anything left to think about that day and I started making notes for the part of the story I was working on. I had actually started thinking of it as a real book. I wrote down some things that I remembered about when we went to the adult toy store in Las Vegas and tried to figure how to work that in to the rest of the story. By the time I finished my last french fry I had an outline, two or three paragraphs and a few lines to remind me of some of the things that happened that I wanted to include later. I went back to work with my mind replaying the whole scene over and over. Through the afternoon I found myself stopping at odd times to make a note on a three by five card I carried in my back pocket.

When I got home I found a note from Tangee telling me to go ahead and eat dinner because she was out with Camay. Probably they were shopping for Ground Hog Day decorations for the house, I thought. I zapped a frozen dinner and took a shower. As I dried off I saw the three by five card sticking out of the back pocket of my jeans. I went to my computer and typed up what I had written. Then I printed it and read it and started a new document. The words just fell of the ends of my fingers. It was like I could see pictures of everything I wanted to write and everything I saw came out on the page. Within two hours I had written over two thousand words. I printed it and read it and decided it was pretty good. Maybe this *could* get to be a real book.

I went into the living room and found a book I'd read a few months ago. It was a novel about this architect who had given up his business and moved to Alaska and all of the things that had happened to him up there. I opened the book and found a page in the middle of a chapter. I counted the words in several lines on the page. Then I counted the number of lines on the page. I did this for a few other pages. There were about three hundred pages in the book and I did some multiplying. By my best guess there were about ninety thousand words in that story. I had just written a thousand words in two hours. That meant that if I wrote eight hours a day I could finish my book in about three and a half weeks. With working and everything I knew I couldn't do that, but four hours a day might not be too hard and then I could work on it full days on the weekends. Maybe I could have it done in eight or ten weeks. Then I could sell it to a publisher and by Christmas I could give copies of my new book to all my friends for presents. I turned on the TV to watch the end of the hockey game and start thinking up designs for the book's cover. I also wondered about what I'd wear for the picture they would use on the back of the book. I hoped they wouldn't make me wear a tie.

The next week didn't go so well. Some lumber that I'd ordered at work was the wrong size, one of the guys who worked for me quit, and my stomach had started giving me nasty, acidy little burps for two hours after I ate my lunchburgers. I hadn't written a word.

I wondered if my writing was making any sense so I left a copy of what I'd done so far on the kitchen table in a big manila envelope with a note for Tangee to read it and tell me what she thought. I had to leave her notes because her part-time job was becoming more full time all the time. The next afternoon I found she was using my story and my note as a place mat for her Christmas cactus, which she was in the process of repotting.

That evening I asked her, "Tangee, I left an envelope on the table. How come the envelope's under your Christmas cactus?"

"To keep the dirt from coming out the little hole in the bottom," she said.

Except for her Bible I'd never seen Tangee actually read a book ever in her life. She'd scan the tabloids and she had to do some reading at the TV station, but it was silly of me to have expected her to be much of a critic, or even to be very interested. I took the envelope back to my writing room.

I put the envelope down and decided to sort through the mail. I threw out everything except the phone bill and the newspaper.

I don't generally read the big city newspapers. We have a weekly paper, The Huron Bay Beacon, that comes to the house every Wednesday. It's a whole lot more than a shopping guide but a whole lot less than The New York Times, although The Times doesn't tell you about the bad accident you saw last week. The Times doesn't print pictures and stories about people you know who are getting engaged and getting new jobs and getting dead. And it doesn't have our classified ads and it doesn't have a full-page column on local events and clubs. Our paper does.

I was planning to sell my lawn tractor and thought I'd see how much people were selling them for. Facing the classified ads page was the clubs and events page. The first item read, "The bi-monthly meeting of The Southeast Columbus County Writer's Group has changed its meeting dates from the second and fourth Tuesday of the month to the first and third Thursday. Meetings start at seven P. M. in the community room of Beverly's Books in the Columbus Shopping Mall. All writers are welcome." This sounded good. I could get together with real writers and maybe they could give me pointers on how to do my story. It wouldn't be like a class. I wouldn't have assignments or boring lectures. I decided to go. The next meeting was tomorrow.

The community room at Beverly's Books turned out to be a back storeroom with a long table in the middle and unfinished drywall all around. A stained, ivory colored coffeemaker sat on a corner table and burped quietly as the pot filled. As I walked in the ten women and three men were just sitting down.

"Writer's Group?" I asked. They smiled and nodded and found me a folding wooden chair that they scrunched in at one corner of the table for me. I sat down.

There were announcements and minutes of the last meeting and old business and new business. There was a rather heated discussion about whether Cookie Duty should continue to be rotated or if it should be assigned on a quarterly basis. Quarterly won by a narrow margin. I didn't vote. Nearly an hour had passed. We took a break. Nobody had mentioned writing. I was about to go back to my car and head home when one of the men from the meeting approached.

"Hi," he said. "Don't mind Linda Lou. The regular president, Judy Marks, is in Mexico. Cancun, I think. Linda Lou likes things to be very official. I'm Clement."

I introduced myself and asked if we were going to talk about writing later. Clement assured me that we would, so I decided to stay. Clement had that fidgety, dancing look in his eye that either meant that he had to piss real bad or that he was a smoker. I patted my shirt pocket and said, "I'm going to step outside for a few minutes." He smiled a relieved smile and I followed him out to an alcove, just outside the back door of the shop. We lit up.

"No place left for a civilized man to get a smoke anymore," he said, drawing deep.

"Well," I said, "it *is* a bookstore."

"I remember when you could smoke in a bookstore or in a drugstore or in a grocery store or anywhere." Clement was a few years older than me. "Hell," he went on, "I remember when my father had his heart attack we were all smoking right in his room."

I said, "What kind of things do you like to write?"

"I don't like to write anything," he said. "I hate writing. It makes me nervous and edgy and my back hurts when I sit at the computer too long. Also I'm a lousy typist and I get mad when I go so slow."

"Okay," I said, "so what kinds of things do you hate to write but that you write anyway? And if you hate it, why do it?"

He said, "I really dislike poetry. I try to limit myself to two or three a week, and I keep the damn things short. Short stories are worse. They have to make sense which poetry doesn't unless you want it to. Novels are the worst. God, the number of hours you can spend just plotting and typing and rewriting and replotting. Gives me a headache just to think about it."

"But you do it anyway? Like, it's something you feel compelled to do?"

"Your name is Buck, isn't it?" I nodded. "Buck, it's simple. Writing these damn things is the only way for me to get them out of my head. If I don't write them down the way I know they have to be, they just keep clanging around inside my head like the bells in a carillon. After I write them and they're on paper it's like I've trapped them and they're outside of my head and I can forget them."

"Huh," I said. "I don't…"

"You don't get it do you?" said Clement. "Well, that's a good thing. Pray you never do."

"No," I said. "I get it. It's like watching a movie in your brain and it keeps looping over and over, changing a little bit here and a little bit there, and it just keeps looping until you make it into a story and tell somebody. Or write it, I guess."

"Damn," said Clement, "you do get it. But you started to say that you didn't…?"

"Oh. I was just going to say that I didn't think I'd ever heard anybody use the word 'carillon' in a regular sentence before."

"You should write humor, Buck. What do you write anyway?"

"Just about things that happen."

Linda Lou called from the doorway and we rejoined the group for the second half of the meeting. Clement moved his briefcase next to mine and we shared the far end of the table.

"Our assignment," began Linda Lou, "was to write our five hundred words on a special subject and that subject was to do with a wall." She looked around the group with a hopeful, fifth grade English teacher look. "Who would like to start?"

Assignments. I should have known there'd be assignments.

"Don't worry about it," said Clement. "It's not like you get a failing grade if you don't do it."

"Now Clement," said Linda Lou, "don't go discouraging our new member." She smiled at me. "These are not really assignments," she said in my direction. "They're more like exercises. Ways to use your writing muscles. You'll see. You'll like them. Now…who will be first to read?" No one volunteered. "Becky," she said, "I know you've brought something."

Becky looked nervous. I guessed her to be about thirty-five, but she had these forty-five year old lines around her eyes. Her hands looked older than that. She smiled a brave little smile and said, "It's not much. Just a few things…not even a proper story, really. It's from the book I'm writing but it had to do with a wall, kind of. I can wait until last." She fumbled around in her tan canvass tote bag while she spoke. Then she looked up and plopped a pound and a half of lined paper on the table. "But I guess I can read now if you want."

"You remember last time I read? Where Carmine and Angela were being stranded in a castle during the French Civil War? And Carmine had to get to his father's country estate to deliver the King's message? This part is from when he's in the castle." She cleared her throat, adjusted her glasses and started reading. Thirty minutes later she was still going at it. Carmine was behind the castle wall, dodging machine gun fire and lobbing grenades. She turned another page and cleared her throat giving Clement just enough time to say, "Becky, don't you want to save some time for our feedback?"

Becky looked at her watch and considered. "I only have eight or ten pages to go in this section. But I guess I could stop here. So, what do you think? I know it's not much."

"It's garbage." A large dark man sitting in an armchair off to the side of the table unfolded his arms. No one looked shocked. He flapped a hand at Becky and repeated, "Garbage. Not that I mean that in a bad way. Light, fluffy, inaccurate, romantic, commercial bullshit," he said. Becky nodded earnestly. "The kind of garbage that would sell a quarter million copies in three weeks and wind up on some celebrities booklist."

"Honestly Warden," said Linda Lou, "I'm sure you could find a more constructive way to state your feelings."

"Garbage is constructive. Bullshit is constructive. One need only be bright enough to appreciate the useful nature of my critique."

"Warden, you are rude," this from a very pretty redhead seated next to Becky. "You've never been published. Not even one of your nasty little short stories. What gives you the right to say things like that to Becky when she's obviously worked so hard?"

"What gives me the right? Me?" Warden's voice was moving higher. His face was red. "I have the right to critique anybody's writing I damn well feel like. Why? Because I'm a reader. It doesn't take a writer to know good writing…it takes a reader to know good writing." He was almost shouting. "And I know garbage when I hear it." He turned toward Becky, jabbed a forefinger at the manuscript and said in a much softer voice, "Now that part about the ivy and how it covered the wall…that was well written. Do more of that." He was quiet and smiling now. "It's garbage, but it's well done."

Several other people read. One woman had a poem that described the wall between sinners and Jesus and how He's given them a ladder to climb that wall. Everyone told her how lovely her poem was. I even nodded my head even though the thing had been awful. It seemed like the right thing to do but I hoped that if I ever read anything for the group I might hear something more useful than "garbage" and "lovely".

The meeting broke up around nine-thirty and Clement asked if I'd like to get a cup of coffee with him and Warden. We occupied a booth at the nearby Family Diner until nearly eleven. We talked about everything from politics to religion and even mentioned writing a time or two. "Will you be at the next meeting?" asked Warden.

"Yeah, I think so," I said, "but I'm not sure about writing the assignment. We have to write five hundred words on 'Going Down the Road?'"

"You don't have to," said Clement. "But why not. I find these exercises useful. Not for the stories themselves, but for the ideas I get while I write them. Try it."

"Yes," said Warden, "I'd like to see what you could do with that subject."

"Well, okay," I said, "but I'd sure rather be getting help on the book I'm writing."

"Bring that too," said Warden. "We'll look at it here at the diner after the meeting."

I had hoped to tell Tangee about the club but when I got home she was already in bed asleep. I had to wait until the next morning.

"It's good you have this club to go to," she said.

"Yeah. I hope they can help me with the book. It's going pretty good but there are lots of things about writing something like that that I need to learn."

"It's a nice hobby for you," she said.

Hobby? I hadn't thought of it as being a hobby. It was a project. It was a whole other occupation.

"A hobby," I said. "Like you have your little hobby working down at the TV station." That sounded mean, but I kind of felt mean. "And besides," I went on, "writing is hard work."

"My job at the station is a job. It's a real job and they pay me real money and they listen to me. And I do too know that writing is hard work."

"I don't know how you know that," I said. "You've never even read the things I'm writing."

"I know that, Buck Crimmins, because I write all my own stories at the station. I do my own research and my own fact checking and I sit at my computer at work and write every word I say on the air. And I've never read your stories maybe because you've never asked me to." I didn't even mention that I'd left a copy in an envelope for her to read. Maybe she wanted an engraved invitation.

We didn't say much more while we finished our coffees. Then

she kissed me goodbye and left for work. We were both mad and I didn't know why.

Before I left for work I sealed another copy of my story in a big envelope and put it on the dining table. I put a big note on top of it, "Dear Tangee, I would like very much to have your opinion of my manuscript. Let me know what you think when you get a chance. Love Buck." That was as close to an engraved invitation as she was going to get.

When I got home I found a note from Tangee, "Bucky, It's really very nice but a little hard to read sometimes. Love Tangee."

Hard to read? I picked up the envelope. It hadn't even been opened.

I opened the envelope and reread the story. I didn't think it was hard to read at all. Tangee had been the wrong one to ask. I decided to take it to writer's group for the next meeting. I'd ask Clement or Warden to read it at the diner. For the meeting itself I was supposed to write a story or something about, "Going Down the Road." That seemed like a very hard subject. I couldn't think of any kind of story about going down a road. I thought about it for most of the next two weeks and didn't come up with much. Just a whole bunch of parts of ideas, but all of them were very different from one another. Then the night before the meeting I had an idea. I'd write that whole bunch of little stories and tie them together. It might make sense like that.

I found Clement smoking behind the bookstore.

"You came back," he said, smiling.

"Yup. I thought I'd give it another try."

"Did you bring something?"

"About 'Going Down the Road'? Yeah, I brought something, but I'm not sure if it really fits what they have in mind."

"They," Clement nodded to the bookstore, "don't have much of anything in mind. Don't worry. You'll do fine." He flicked his cigarette butt toward the parking lot, just missing the curb. Linda Lou called us from the doorway and I flicked my butt, clearing the curb by a good foot and a half. Clement nodded appreciatively. We went in.

The business part of the meeting didn't take too long this time. Olive was voted an extra three dollars from the treasury for postage. Then we read our Going Down the Road stories. I had planned on going last because I was pretty shy about reading my story out loud. I'd never read anything I'd written out loud before.

Olive was first. "I have a poem," she said. I heard Warden grind his teeth. Olive read about life as a road of sadness with happiness on either side. I think she meant to deal with turning off the road to find the happiness you want, but the way she did it made it sound like turning off the straight and narrow road was suicidal. It wasn't terribly clear. I watched the other writers as she read. A few stared at her and nodded when they thought she'd made a point. Mostly they sat with their eyes squinted shut. I believe they intended to look like they were intensely interested, but the overall effect was that they had group constipation, or maybe just gas. When she finished, folks picked out words and images from the poem and said how they liked it. I think they were desperately trying to sound helpful and nice, not so much out of interest or kindness, but because they would each be reading soon and hoped to hear nice words too. Warden had sucked his lips into his mouth and was biting hard to keep from talking.

Clement read a beautiful little story about a path going past an ancient wall, and the fellow who walked that path every day as a child and his sense of wonder about what was on the other side. It didn't have much of a point but the writing was wonderful. I wanted to ask what it was about but I didn't have the nerve. Everybody told Clement how lovely his story was. He said thank you but didn't seem pleased.

Then it was my turn. I wanted to explain how I wrote the story and that I hoped everyone would understand that I was pretty new to all this, but I decided I'd just read. I had made copies and passed them out. Then I took a breath and started. This is what I read.

* * *

GOING DOWN THE ROAD
By Buck Crimmins

I tried. I really tried, but the harder I tried the worse it got. Writer's block. Last week I gave up looking for an original story idea and decided to ask some friends and relatives for their ideas or inspiration for the subject, "Going Down the Road." The following is what I got. Please accept this offering in lieu of an original story.

My friend, C. T. (Clarence) Bunn, was retarded long before Forrest Gump made it cool. I told him my subject, turned on my recording machine, and C. T. said,
"Going Down the Road.
I would buy a car, get a fast car,
Gonna drive it down the road.
I will drive it fast.
And I will get a car that's fast;
and red and pretty
but I don't mind rust
if the air don't get in.
I'm gonna go down the road to…
to…
to where I want to…
maybe to Bennies.
I could go to MacDonald's and I could go by myself and go to the drive up place and drink an orange drink by the bridge.
And give fries to them white birds."
C. T. may be slow, but sometimes he can be really, really clear.

Russell Stokes worked in the steel mills in Gary, Indiana for forty years before he moved to Columbus Township. He said, "You could write like, philosophy. You could use all them big words. You could do that. Like, you know, 'Life is Like a Road,' and as to how we're all just going down this here road and the different stops we make. But you know, life's not like a road. Life is really like a Super 8 Motel. No pool, no room service, and you have to check out a whole lot sooner than you'd like."

My Uncle Vern was only half sober when I spoke with him and so it makes perfect sense that he came up with barely half a story, starting in the middle and not quite ending it. He said, "So, after striking out with the six most affordable harlots at Spike's Keg-O-Nails Tavern, Andy left. He ran into Alonzo, the dogcatchers dog, who was even more amorously deprived and desperate than Andy and proceeded to hump his right leg whilst being dragged near twenty yards down the road. That is to say, it was Alonzo doing the humping, not Andy, who had yet to find a suitable humpee-at least not one of his own species."

Elizabeth Archer runs a checkout lane at Kroger's, wishes she had finished school, claims to have twenty-seven original ideas for romance novels in the back of her mind, and just might come to our next meeting. She said, "Down the road? Well, really, do you mean a road or a street or a boulevard or just what? And are we being metaphorical here or rather more descriptive. I once wrote an essay on spring wildflowers along the unpaved and semi-improved roads of eastern Huron County. Would something like that count?" If you see her here in July, don't encourage her.

Dave was twenty-one when certain of my friends and I were nineteen, and as such was our close friend, best buddy and buyer of beer and harsh spirits. I've kept in touch with him ever since then. He told me, "The road. The road is Woodward Avenue; U.S. 10, 1963. We rode that road a quarter mile at a time; drive-in to drive-in and drag racing at every stop light in between. Knock the hub caps off Dad's Chevy and pretend to be cool. That was the road. Now it's I-94 and the mini-van; no more pretending. Thirty years past cool."

Well, there you have it, five hundred some odd words for our subject of Going Down the Road. I just wish more of them had been my own.

***

I finished reading and I was breathless. My ears were ringing and my heart was beating hard. I know I'd read it way too fast because a couple of times Clement had to tell me to slow down. But I remembered that I had meant it to be funny and that people had laughed in all the right places. That was nice.

Then Linda Lou said, "Buck, that was very nice. And funny. Didn't you all think it was funny in places?" Everybody nodded. Everybody had big smiles. "But, usually most of what we all write here is fiction. I'm sure this was a fun exercise for you, using your recorder and everything, but couldn't you have taken one of these things that people told you and written a story about it? In your own words? Made up your own dialog? It might not have been as funny as what these people really said, but at least it would have been original."

She didn't believe I had written my own story. I could feel the redness in my ears. I didn't hardly know what to say. She thought I cheated. I couldn't speak. The room was quiet. Then Warden said, "Well?" He was still smiling. I swallowed. I looked at Linda Lou and found enough breath to speak. "This is a story," I said. "I wrote this last night at ten o'clock. I don't know anybody named C. T. Bunn or any of those other people. It's fiction. It's the first fiction story I've ever written and read out loud. See, the part about it not being a story is part of the story."

"Oh," said Linda Lou.

Several other people read their stories. Linda Lou didn't. Linda Lou didn't say a word the rest of the evening. When the meeting ended people stood around and told me they really liked my story and asked my where I got all the ideas from and things like that. I never saw Linda Lou leave.

"Mister Crimmins," said Warden, "let's us three repair to the diner. We have some writing to talk about."

The diner was a block and a half down from the bookstore. The place hadn't been redecorated since it had been built in the nineteen-thirties and I liked it that way. It even felt comfortable to smoke in there and that's a rare feeling anymore. Elbows had worn the pink pansies on the Formica table top into a blur. I sipped a ginger ale and waited for my Rueben sandwich. Clement and Warden drank coffee.

"Pity they don't serve beer here," said Warden. "After some of those poems I could use a beer."

Clement said, "I've told you before, if you want to meet at a bar, or someplace that has drinks, that's fine with me. Just because I'm an alcoholic doesn't mean you have to be dry."

"This place is fine," said Warden.

"Actually," Clement said to me, "Warden prefers to come here. He's still waiting for Karen, our lovely waitress, to ask him out. I think he figures if he leaves her enough two-dollar tips, she'll beg him to take her back to his apartment."

Our food showed up. Between French fries Clement reviewed my story. "Very nice," he said. "The part about the dog catcher's dog is good. Funny. And the part about C. T. Bunn…that was very different. Clever. Almost poetic in some ways."

Warden nearly choked at the mention of poetry. "It's not a damn poem. It's a stream of consciousness thing. It's not a poem is it?"

"I hadn't meant it to be," I said. "But I've known some people who were kind of like that. Real slow. I guess some would call them retarded. They talked that way. If you just forget that their words don't come out in the regular order they make a lot of sense. I just thought it would be different to try to include that."

"Your transitions between sections need something," said Warden. "It's too abrupt."

We talked for two more hours. I lent them copies of my stories about the road trip to Vegas. We agreed to meet again in two weeks.

Tangee was now on TV every night. She did interviews with local people and did segments showing photos from recent local weddings. She also started reviewing cook books, so I didn't have to cook so much myself and I also got to learn all about tofu. If she talked to somebody who could see angels, she would check out every shadow for two weeks. You never know where you might find an angel.

Everything she researched got to be the most important thing in her life…at least for a while. Then she started a series of interviews with marriage experts. I didn't like that near as well as tofu.

"We need a hobby," she said, one night after work.

"We have a hobby," I said, "it's called life. Living takes darn near twenty-four hours a day. We don't have time for macramé."

"But we need to do something together. I interviewed a man from the Columbus County Marriage and Family Center, and he said that if a husband and wife don't have some fun activity to do together, they are doomed."

"Doomed? He actually said the word 'doomed'? So if we spend an hour every evening tying knots together we'll be un-doomed?"

"Buck, I'm serious. We don't do near enough stuff together anymore."

"Anymore, I come home from work and you're still out talking to people who think the great American marriage is based on making hanging baskets out of twine."

"You're mocking me. I hate when you mock me. It wouldn't have to be macramé. It could be bowling or taking dancing lessons or working in the garden."

"This is silly," I said, "but, okay…you make a list of fun things to do and I'll look at it." Tangee frowned.

Then I suggested a real fun thing we could do together and she suggested that she had a headache and so I suggested she take her headache to bed and let me write for a while. Life was getting complicated.

I decided that I had better write some more about the road trip to Vegas before the two weeks were up. It was fun. I kept a little spiral notebook in my back pocket and whenever I remembered part of the trip, I just made some notes. Then at night I'd look over the notes I'd made and write scenes as I remembered them. I wrote about the night we stayed in the Blue Lake Dump. I wrote about going to The Big Blue X sex store. I wrote about everything, but I wrote it very plain. I didn't put in what any of us said or any description; just a few paragraphs saying what happened.

When I met Clement and Warden next, I showed them what I had done.

"It reads like a damn book report," said Warden. "How I spent my summer vacation."

"Yes," said Clement, "but this is just a first draft isn't it?"

"If that's what you call it," I said. "I mean, I'm going to go back and put other stuff in. It's still kind of an outline."

"Good," said Warden. "Outlines are good. But then what?"

"Then I'm going to string all of the little stories together and re-type them to make into one big story."

"Next time why not bring a few of these stories complete with dialog and everything. By the time you're through with this, it's going to be quite a book."

A book. I really was writing a book. Wow.

We spent the rest of the evening talking about child labor laws in Mexico. I'm not sure why we did that, but I think I learned a lot. Mostly I listened. Mostly I listened while thinking about the idea that I was writing a book.

Our bi-weekly get-togethers became weekly. I felt like I was in a writing class where I was the only student and I had two teachers. I learned how to do dialog and setting and everything so much better than I ever had at my night class. Some weeks I wrote pages and pages. Other weeks I didn't write anything at all, but after a few months when I printed out everything I had written, the paper weighed over a pound. I had written a whole pound of words and altogether they made the story of the road trip.

"Now what?" I asked over Monday evening coffee, after Clement and Warden had had a chance to read it.

"It's a really fun story, Buck," said Warden. "You guys did more in a few days in Las Vegas than most people ever get to do."

Clement said, "So, you actually got to see that show where the two Japanese guys do magic tricks while surrounded by a bunch of Great White Sharks? That must be quite a show."

"Yeah," I said, "they really seem to have a close relationship with those fish."

"Too close," said Warden. "That one guy is supposed to be out of the hospital next month. Mauled by a Great White…that was something."

Clement said, "Well, it was his own fault. I mean he shouldn't have been dangling his one year old son over the tank. He was lucky that the critter just got a chunk of his arm and missed the kid."

"I saw the video of that," I said. "His partner says the boy was in no real danger, though. His dad was holding him at least six feet over the top of the tank. Sharks can't jump out of the water."

"This one did," said Warden. "High enough to get a mouthful of forearm."

Clement said, "The people from the casino said the shark probably thought the baby was attacking his father. Some kind of protective instinct."

"I think it was more of a lunch instinct, but who knows?"

"Well," said Clement, "It's too long for a short story and too short for a book. Maybe it's a section of a book. Have you had any other experiences that you could write up like this?"

I thought that my life with Tangee had been full of experiences, but I doubted that anybody else would want to read about them. Then I mentioned Tangee's Plastiqueen party and what happened after that.

"Write it," said Warden. I wrote it. It took three months and lots of coffee, but I wrote it. Actually it took more like ten or twenty hours to write, but the problem was that after I'd written a few pages in a few hours, I was done for a while. It was like I had squeezed as much of the story out of me as I could and had to wait for some more to build up again.

While all of this writing was going on, Tangee was becoming a celebrity. People stopped us to say how much they liked her segment. Actually, people stopped her to talk about that. I got to stand there and smile while she signed autographs. Her ninety second spot on Thursdays had turned into five full minutes, three days a week and I guess there was talk of her getting her own regular, half-hour program. Part of her success was her enthusiasm.

I came home from work one Wednesday and was in kind of a hurry to get to the bathroom. I rounded the corner from the hall and whanged into a big blue plastic wheel mounted against the doorframe. On the opposite doorframe was another big blue plastic wheel.

"Tangee," I hollered, "why are there two big blue plastic wheels mounted on this doorframe? I could have broke my shoulder."

"They're Muscle-izers," she called from the kitchen. "Be careful."

I came into the kitchen rubbing my shoulder and said, "It's hard to be careful of something that you don't even know is there to be careful of."

"Well, I'm sorry. I would have told you, but I didn't see you when you came in."

"Muscle-izers?"

"It's a thing this man invented for exercise. See?" I followed her to the doorframe and she stood between the wheels, grabbing a small handle in each hand. Then she flailed around for a minute looking like a lawn whirligig in a strong breeze.

"I'm going to be interviewing the inventor and I had to try them out first. They're not really much fun after the first few times, but I guess it's supposed to get rid of all this flab up here." She held out her arm and pointed to her absolutely flabless upper arm.

"So, now I have to slow down before I make my right turn to the bathroom for the rest of my life?"

"Maybe two weeks," she said. "That's how long you have to use it before you see results."

"But you don't need results. You have pretty, skinny arms."

"Still, I have to do the interview, and I have to know."

I remembered why I had been in a hurry and went to the bathroom.

She was that way about everything. She couldn't have just looked at the Muscle-izer brochure and then interviewed the guy. She had to use the thing.

I still had a big old bruise on my arm when I met Clement and Warden the following Monday. I explained about Muscle-izers.

"That's another story you could write about," said Clement.

"Who would care about two plastic wheels and a big old bruise?" I asked.

"You just seem to have experiences that other people don't have," said Warden. "Life in your house must be fun."

"Not fun like it used to be," I said. "Before Tangee was on TV I think it was a lot more fun."

"Don't like her being the center of attention?"

"No, it's not that," I said. "It's just that now she's interested in a lot of other things that mostly I don't care about. But it's okay. I just let her do her TV thing and I do my work forty hours and keep the house up and cook dinner and write thing. In fact, we hardly see each other for more than an hour at a time anymore. But it's okay."

"So," said Clement. "How much writing have you actually done? I mean on the book."

I said, "Sixty-one thousand, four hundred and twenty two words." I loved the word count feature of my word processing program. Every time I finished writing, I'd check to see how far I'd come. It was kind of like checking the gas mileage on my truck whenever I'd fill up. It was like measuring the snow before I shoveled it. It was like counting the number of cigarettes I smoked every day. Progress. Milestones. Like that.

"Really?" said Warden. "Buck, that's a whole book, a small one, but a still a book. I hadn't realized that you'd done quite so much."

"Yeah," I said. "I know. So, now what?"

"Now you send it out."

"To a real publisher?"

"Yes, to a real publisher. You borrow my copy of American Writer's Sourcebook and find a publisher and send it out. I have it in my briefcase in my car. You can take it tonight. The Sourcebook has listings for every single book publisher in the country and the kind of books they publish and even what they pay. And while your looking up publishers this week, I'll go over what you've written and do a bit of editing. We've already seen most of it, I think, but I want to read the whole thing, start to finish and make sure you haven't missed any little things."

That night, with Sport Center playing in the background on the TV, I started looking through the Sourcebook. There were over two-hundred listings and it seemed like most of them weren't very interested in writers sending their stories to them. They wanted stories sent by agents. I didn't have an agent and had no idea where I'd find one. But there were a number of publishers who would still accept something sent right from the writer.

In the back of the Sourcebook I also found an index that showed the subjects that each publisher wanted to see. I had to decide from the topics where I fit in. I guessed I might be, "Mainstream and General," but that sounded too general. And mainstream. Everybody said my stories were funny but there was no category marked, "Funny," or even, "Comedy." Funny would have been okay, but I wasn't sure I wanted my life to be called a comedy. Then I saw the Humor listing. It was the section right below Gay and Lesbian, but not as big. Not half as big. There were fifteen publishers specializing in Gay and Lesbian stories and seven specializing in Humor. I thought about that for a while and although the idea that there seemed to be a wide interest in homosexuality was not surprising, it did kind of bother me that there was only half as much interest in humor.

I read each of the Humor entries and found only two that would look at my story without an agent. One of them was only interested in Gay and Lesbian humor. The other was called Green Barn Press. I liked the name of that publisher. I liked the idea of a green barn and decided that if I ever had a barn I'd paint it green. Especially if they bought my book.

I typed up a letter to send with my story and took it with me to the diner to show Clement and Warden.

"For a guy who writes good stories, you sure write a crappy letter," said Warden. Clement nodded.

"What's wrong with it?" I asked. "It's short and it's to the point. I don't want to waste Ms. Carrie Cannoway's time. She's the editor. She'll read the book. If she likes it she'll buy it."

"Looking at this letter is hardly going to entice her into reading your book. Listen," Warden picked up my letter and read it out loud.

"Dear Ms. Cannoway; The enclosed book is called Buck and Tangee: Things that Happened. It is a book of humor. Please read it and consider it for publication. Sincerely, Buck Crimmins."

"So what's wrong with that? I think it's perfect," I said, feeling a little flushed at the critique. I didn't mind Clement and Warden helping with my stories. It was real helpful. But this was a two line letter.

Clement said, "There's no hook, so spark, no nothing. It's just here's my book. The person is going to read this and say, if this book is as humorous as the letter, forget it."

They noted lots of suggestions for me to include when I rewrote the letter, but when I got home I took my typed up story and my original letter and put them in a file and sent it off to Green Barn Press.

Two months later I still hadn't heard from Green Barn. I also hadn't heard much from Tangee. She was getting more and more involved with her TV thing. I just let her do it. I really didn't understand much about what went on down at the station, but then she didn't understand many of the finer points of constructing tiny buildings. I figured it was just one of those times in a marriage when the married people do their own thing for a while.

One Tuesday I found her sitting at the kitchen table tearing a paper napkin into long thin strips.

"Craft project for your show?" I asked, trying to sound interested.

"No. I'm just thinking."

"Okay."

"Aren't you going to ask what I'm thinking about?" she asked.

"Probably something about your show. You know I don't know much about all that."

"Yes," she said, "I know. I'm thinking about the interview I did today."

"Was it good?" I asked.

"It was interesting," she said. "You didn't see it did you?"

"No," I said. "I meant to, but my TV at work isn't working so good." My TV at work is working fine. I just don't usually have the time to sit and watch Tangee talk to some guy about his haunted house, or somebody else who'd just written a book on how to raise your kids.

"Do you want me to send out for a pizza?" I asked.

She looked at me for a long minute and then said, "No, I'll get something at Camay's."

"I didn't know you were even going to your sister's tonight, but okay. I'll just make something for myself."

Tangee got home a little after eleven and went up to bed. I stayed up until after one, wondering when I'd hear about my story from the people at Green Barn.

The next day was Wednesday, the fifteenth, which I remember real well, because that was the day I got my rejection letter from Green Barn. That was also the day Tangee left me. There was a note.

Dear Buck,
I am living at Camay's house now. Don't worry, I'm fine. I really wish you would have seen my show the other day or even asked about it. I interviewed a professor about this book. I put a copy of it by your TV chair and maybe you can look at it before Sports Center or maybe after Sports Center if you're not too tired. After you look at the book, you'll understand everything and then you can call me. I love you.
Love,
Tangee

I stood there and felt like my head had been whacked by the flat side of a one by four...too startled to feel the pain and too conscious to fall down, but still pretty sure that at least one of those things was about to happen. But I didn't exactly fall. I just sat down...all of a sudden...on the floor. I just kept thinking to myself, "Huh?"

Finally my head cleared enough to remember Camay's phone number.

"Yes, Buck, she's here, and no, you can't talk to her."

"Come on, Camay, just put her on the phone," I said.

"Tangee says that after you read the book, then you can call."

There was a brief pause and I knew Tangee was telling her something. "And don't even think about coming over. Not until you read the book."

"I wasn't even thinking of coming over," I lied. Then we were both uncomfortably quiet for a few seconds. "Tell her," I said, "that I'm going to read the book. And there better be some pretty good answers in there too." I hung up.

I grabbed a can of Coke and sat down in my TV chair. I left the TV off; this was going to be some serious reading. On the little table next to me was a hard cover book. It was called, "A Separate Marriage," by Dr. Franklin Pewamic. I read the blurb on the front fly-leaf to see what I was in for.

The first thing I found out was that Dr. Franklin Pewamic was a woman. I wasn't even the littlest bit surprised. Dr. Pewamic had spent the last dozen years living with various tribes and tribal families all over the world, but mostly in the Amazon rain forest and on some Pacific islands. After all that time and hours of video and tons of notes, she had figured out that there were some marital habits that would be good for Americans to learn. I turned to chapter one. It was boring. So was chapter two. Mostly she was writing about marriage in America and the divorce rate and all the things she thought were wrong. Then she talked about how she got her studies funded. Boring. I took a bathroom break. I didn't take the book.

When I came back to my TV chair and went to open the book, I found some tiny slips of paper in it that I hadn't noticed before. Bookmarks. Some of them had Tangee's notes on them. Mostly the notes amounted to smiley faces and exclamation marks. These were the places that Tangee had found interesting. In fact, they may have been the only places that she read. The part of the book I'd just finished was still kind of stiff and new and the pages make a cracking sound when I turned them. These marked pages had been read and there were even some underlines.

The places Tangee seemed to have liked best were all descriptions of jungle married life. The first thing I noticed was that many of the tribes were headed by women. Dr. Pewamic was sure this contributed to stability. The thing they all had in common was that the husbands and wives lived in separate places from each other. In some tribes each woman had her own hut. In others, all of the men lived in one lodge and the wives lived in another. In all of them, everybody was happy. The Doctor concluded that if American husbands and wives lived separately, they would get along much better.

After I read the bookmarked places, I scanned some of the remaining chapters, but mostly they were just very dry analysis of the good parts. The only section that caught my eye and that I read all the way through had to do with Dr. Pewamic joining one particular tribe and taking a few husbands of her own to live apart from. She talked about how satisfying her orgasms were without having to put up with a full time relationship. It might have been scholarly research, but it sounded like an American kid's description of college life.

I read as much of the book as I could in one sitting and called Camay back.

"Hi, it's me," I said.

"Hi, Buck," said Camay. "Just a minute."

I could hear a muffled conversation in the background while I waited. Camay came back on the line, "Did you read the book?"

"I read the book," I said. More muffled conversation.

"Hi, Bucky." Tangee sounded happy to talk to me but maybe a little shy.

"Hi."

"You read the book?"

"Yup."

"Oh, good. I was so worried you'd be mad and not read it. It was so good, wasn't it?"

"I don't know," I said. "I mean, it was all a little odd, I thought. So, tell me, what is this all about? Why are you gone and I'm here and reading this book?" I didn't tell her about the part about feeling whacked by a one by four.

"It's our marriage. We have to save it. Doctor Pewamic says we're in terrible danger."

"Doctor Pewamic doesn't even know us. What danger?"

"She talked to me for a long time after I interviewed her. She says couples like us are in danger. We've been married for so long and you don't cheat on me and you don't do drugs or get drunk and you don't even spend a lot of money gambling and you're writing a book and you love me."

I couldn't think of what to say.

She went on, "And I have always stayed home and now I've got a job I love and I don't have a boyfriend on the side."

"But those are all good things," I said.

"No. Those are only good things for a while. After a long time they get to be bad things. She said it's like a pressure of good things building up and then bang."

"Bang? What bang? Being happily married is going to make us sad? Do you want a boyfriend? Do you think I'm going to start taking drugs because I'm too happy?"

"No! I don't want a boyfriend. But she says we could be too happy now and then all of a sudden we'll get bored with all that happiness and next thing you know, it's divorce. But that never happens with the g'putka people. And that's because when they're married, they don't live together. It's like the happiness is kind of thinned out and doesn't get to a critical level."

"We're critically happy?"

"Yes. Exactly. I'm so glad you read the book and agree."

"Tangee, I read the book, but this is stupid." Tangee didn't say anything. "I don't mean you're stupid. Just this Doctor Pewamic and this book and this whole idea. You need to come home now."

"No," said Tangee. "Camay says I can stay here as long as I want, as long as it's only about a week. Then I'm going to get an apartment. Bucky, I love you so much I can't stand the thought of going back to you and ruining our marriage. You have to understand. We'll still be married. We'll visit each other all the time. Maybe even a few times you might stay with me overnight. That's allowed, but only once a month or so."

"Tangee, come home," I said. "At least you have to come home to get some of your stuff." I figured that once I got her home I could pretty easily convince her that this was all foolishness.

"I have all the stuff I need for my new life," she said.

"Did you pack your Silver Garnet Number 21 nail polish?" It might not have been fair, but I had to hit her where it counted.

"No," she said. "I kind of forgot that. Could you bring it over and give it to Camay for me?"

"No," I said. "I could bring it over, but I wouldn't want to waste my once a month visit. You come here."

"Well, okay, but only if Camay comes with me and I wait at the door while you get my Silver Garnet Number 21. And a few other things."

"No Camay, and none of you just standing at the door. You come home and we sit and we talk and then, if you want, I'll give you your Silver Garnet."

"Okay," she said. "But just for a little while."

An hour later Tangee arrived. She looked tired. I felt tired.

We talked until the middle of the evening, but I just couldn't get her to change her mind. She was going off to live in the women's lodge with Camay and I was supposed to stay in the men's lodge by myself. It didn't seem to matter that the women's lodge was one third occupied by Camay's husband.

A week went by. Sometimes she'd talk to me on the phone, but not often. I spent the evenings fiddling with my book, trying to figure out why Green Barn didn't like it. Then I decided to look on the internet to see if I could find a publisher there that wasn't in the Writer's SourceBook. I found one.

Willoughby Press. It looked like they'd be more than happy to publish my book. I clicked through their site. It turned out that they would be more than happy to publish anybody's book as long as the writer was willing to pay them to do it. I had kind of imagined it would be the other way around. Willoughby was a vanity press. Nobody wants to publish your little book of sonnets? Pay Willoughby, they'll print it. Got a two thousand page history of your family tree? Pay Willoughby. I clicked further into the site.

There was a cost estimator built in to the site. I typed in the number of words in my story and the kind of binding I thought would look good. I chose my paper stock and my type font. I choked when I saw the total. I revised my format. The total was still high. I reduced the number of copies I wanted printed. Any way I worked it, it would cost a bunch of money to have my own book printed. I closed the site and shut off my computer.

The next day was Monday but I skipped Writer's Club and went straight to the diner where I waited for Clement and Warden. They seemed happy to see me. I was happier to see them. I told them what had happened with Tangee and they were about as mystified as I was.

"Your lodge? You've got a lodge and she's got a lodge?" said Clement. I nodded.

"Makes perfect sense to me," said Warden. "Probably would have saved any number of my marriages."

"I don't like it," I said. "Especially when it came the same week as this. I showed them my rejection letter from Green Barn.

"Maybe you should try one of the publishers looking for gay and lesbian material," said Warden.

"Huh?" I said.

"Yeah. Just add a fictional buddy to take on the Las Vegas trip. Have him be gay. They'll love it."

"I can't do that," I said. "These are things that really happened. I can't put a gay guy on the trip. Rusty would kill me. You're joking, right?"

"I'm joking," said Warden. "But I think that would be a smarter move than publishing it yourself."

"At least I wouldn't have to wait two months to hear from Willoughby. I bet they write back the next day. And it won't be with a rejection letter."

"Then go for it," said Clement. Warden gave him a hard look. "Why not? If you've got the money, have them run off a hundred copies. Like you said before, you might not make anything on them, but you've got your Christmas presents all lined up for next year."

I thought about it at home that night and decided Clement was right. I didn't write the book to be a famous author and get interviewed by Terri Gross and be on Oprah and get rich or anything. I did it for fun, and the Christmas present thing was just a bonus. The next day I didn't bother to write to Willoughby, I just called them. They said they'd send me an information kit and as soon as I sent it back with my story and a check, I'd be a published writer. That was delayed for a little while when Tangee came home.

"Camay was serious," she said, standing in our kitchen with her suitcase and bags on the floor at her feet. "She said it was time for me to go. Now I don't have a lodge."

I was worried for a minute that she meant I'd have to go find my own lodge, which was something I wasn't going to do. I already have a mortgage on one lodge and I wasn't going to pay rent to live in somebody else's lodge.

"Well," I said, "it looks like we're living in the same lodge together."

"There's another way," said Tangee. "Huts."

"Huts?"

"Some of the tribes don't live in lodges, they live in huts. They are like little houses all gathered around. Sometimes there's a big thatched roof over all of the little huts."

"Sounds like a motel to me."

Tangee considered. "Not exactly, but you get the idea."

"What?"

"This half of the house is my hut," she made a sweeping motion with her arm. "My hut starts at the stairs and goes up to the big bedroom and the big bathroom and the landing. You're hut is over there." She pointed to the back hall. There was my office, the spare bedroom and the three-quarter bath. "We'll have to share the kitchen and the living room. Some tribes do that."

I talked to her and I reasoned with her and I negotiated with her, but she wouldn't change her mind. I'm a lot bigger than Tangee and could have easily settled things by just doing what I wanted to do, but I always hated guys who pushed their wives around like that. I figured that if I was patient, eventually this idea would run its course and she'd get bored with it and things would get back to normal. I told her the hut thing was only a temporary trial. She seemed satisfied and went upstairs with her bags. I was left to wonder who'd get custody of the remote for the big TV in the living room.

I was about to fill out the papers from Willoughby Press and found myself wanting to ask Tangee what she thought about it, but I couldn't do that because she was making us live in huts. I just did it myself, wrote the check and sent it off, along with my story.

A few weeks later a big brown truck dropped off six cases of books on my front porch.

I had forgotten that the bed in the spare bedroom was nasty to sleep on. It was a hard little single bed with a hard lump right in the small of my back. I was used to sleeping on a big, fluffy, queensized bed with Tangee in the small of my back. That was one thing that made the time go slow. Another thing was The Schedule. Tangee had posted a calendar of events on the kitchen wall. Lots of days had coded little messages to tell us what our tribe was doing and on what day. Violet stars meant I had to go grocery shopping. Green stars meant I had to look on the table and take Tangee's prescription bottles to the drug store to be refilled. Red dots were trash day. Smiley faces were for sex. I could tell a month ahead what nights were going to be sex nights. A smiley face with an exclamation mark after it meant that Tangee would be off work at noon and if I came home then we could have sex without waiting for nighttime. I didn't like the smiley faces. Tangee and I had always enjoyed sex whenever we wanted to and I resented seeing not only that we wouldn't be doing anything for the middle four days of the week, but also that on the fifth day it was expected. Not that I even didn't show up for our scheduled sex time, and not that it wasn't good. It's always good. It was just that it seemed so mechanical. But still good. The times I wanted to do something with her on the spur of the moment, she'd tell me I should have requested a schedule modification.

She didn't show any signs of getting bored with our life in a hut. I even did some research on my own and found out some information that Dr. Franklin Pewamic hadn't bothered to put in her book. The internet told me that the tribe where the doctor spent the most time only had eighty-seven members. When asked why husbands and wives preferred to live in separate lodges, I turned out that the words "husband" and "wife" had very different meanings to them. First of all, it was the wife who was married to one man. The man was married to the entire tribe of women. When the men were asked why they didn't prefer monogamy, they laughed. One senior elder said, "Why many women? Why not? They all the same. It like being with one woman." The women found the idea of monogamy interesting. They also liked the radical idea of one man and one wife living in one house. Dr. Pewamic hadn't mentioned that part, but Tangee didn't care. I showed her all the research I had done, but all she said was, "That's not what Franklin told me."

After having my books delivered, I started on my Christmas list and found that there were only about fifteen people I usually exchange gifts with and some of them were in my "under ten dollar" category. My nice, new books had cost one whole lot more than that.

Clement told me, "Marketing. If you want people to read your book, you have to market it."

"Like advertising?"

"Sure. Run an ad in the local paper. Somebody might buy one. Give a couple to the library. They'll probably put it on that front shelf they have for local writers. Ask the bookstore if they'll carry it. There are lots of ways to try to get some interest generated."

The last time I tried to generate some interest in a plan of mine was BaitKing and that didn't turn out too good, but I thought Clement had some good ideas and when Warden agreed with Clement, I knew there was something to it. Warden tells it like it is. I gave them both a copy.

"Sign mine, 'To Warden Burtch, the last great curmudgeon, and brilliant writer in his own right.'" When I finished the inscription Warden said, "This is what you need to do. You need to have a book signing."

"At the library?" I asked.

"No. At least not at first. Go on down to the bookstore and tell them you'll give them a fifty percent discount on books they order from you, if they let you do a signing. You can sit at a card table and talk to people about your book and when they buy it you autograph it for them."

"I wouldn't have to talk to a crowd, would I?" Public speaking was not one of my favorite things.

"No, you could just talk to people one on one. I mean, let's face it, there's probably not going to be a line out the door. And besides, it would be good practice. Maybe the newspaper might interview you."

"Okay," I said. At least the Shade Tree Bookstore and the local shopping news weren't Oprah and Terri Gross.

It turned out that the Shade Tree Bookstore was happy to have me sign books. The owner even smiled politely when I told her about the fifty percent discount. I could tell she wasn't planning on a line out the door either.

My book signing day was the following Saturday. I brought my own table, but the Shade Tree Bookstore lady already had one for me to use, complete with a white table cloth and sign that read, "Shade Tree Welcomes Buck Crimmins, Author of 'Buck and Tangee: Things that Happened'" I planned on staying there from their ten o'clock opening until maybe four in the afternoon with a break for lunch in the middle.

Between opening and ten-thirty only three customers came in. I spent my time practicing my signature on a piece of scrap paper. When I had that down pretty good, I flipped through the pages of the book. The cover wasn't quite what I had planned. I thought a good design would be to have the cover dark blue on the top and tan on the bottom. In tan letters in the upper part would be the name of the book and in blue letters on the bottom would be my name. When it was delivered from Willoughby it was red and black with some swirly orange lines along the side that might have been flames. Willoughby cut forty-two dollars from my bill for the mistake.

Around quarter to eleven a man came into the store with two kids. They went off to the back of the store and he stopped at my table. He picked up a copy of the book and looked at the back and the spine and then he opened it in the middle. I tried to get a look at the section he was reading, but I couldn't tell. It kind of bothered me that he started in the middle. I went to a lot of work to get everything in order. Then he flipped a few pages and said, "Hmm." Then he put the book down and went to join his kids.

By two o'clock I was beginning to question the intelligence of the customers of that book shop. At least three separate times a person came up to me and said, "Did you write this book?" There was a sign sitting right next to me with my name and picture on it, along with a stack of books. Who else would I have been? But I was polite.

Actually, more people stopped by my table to ask if I was Tangee's husband. They asked lots of questions about her, but not much about me. One of them just asked, "Are you Tangee Crimmin's husband?" I said yes. Then he said, "And you wrote this book?" I said yes. He bought a copy and as he left the store he was actually starting to open it. I could see him reading as he walked to his car. That was odd, but at least I'd made a sale. By the end of the day it was the only sale I made.

"You never know how things are going to turn out," said Warden the next time we met. "Things take time." But as it turned out, not much time.

Two days later, Tangee came home just as I was starting to clatter some pans around for dinner. She said, "You don't have to make dinner tonight. We're going out." I checked the calendar but I didn't see any yellow triangles that would have meant we were going out. This was something spontaneous and therefore good. "We're going to have dinner. A business dinner." Not quite as good. My gut got tight. I wondered if this was how a wife asked her husband for a divorce.

"What kind of business?" I asked.

"You'll see." She smiled. Not any kind of mean, I'm-going-to-ask-you-for-a-divorce smile. It was a real one like I hadn't seen for a while. Maybe my days in my hut were going to be over.

We went to a very nice place about ten miles from the house. I'd never been there before. It was close to the TV station. Tangee had her briefcase.

She ordered wine and I got a beer. I didn't know she liked wine, but she ordered it by name just like she knew what she was doing.

We chatted for a bit, but I couldn't stand the wait. "So, what's up? What kind of business dinner is this, anyway." I took a slug of beer and tightened my jaw for the worst.

"You're going to be on my show," said Tangee.

"What?"

"On my show. Next Tuesday, if that's okay with you."

"Why would you want me on your show? To talk about how I build little photo mart buildings and outhouses?"

"No, silly. To talk about your book."

I must have had a totally stupid look on my face. "You're an author," she said, "and I interview authors. And exercise people and psychics and everything, too, but also people who write books. And you wrote a book, and you're local and you're married to me and so it's perfect. Elliot loves the idea. And he likes your book, too."

"Did you tell him about it?" I asked.

"No. He bought it. At the bookstore, the day you were there."

That one guy who bought my book had been Elliot Schurmer, the news anchor at Tangee's station. Things take time. Things also take funny turns.

At first I was all modest and told Tangee that it wasn't a real book and there were only a hundred copies of it and there were probably lots better writers she should have on instead of me. "It's just because I'm your husband, isn't it?" I asked.

"Well, that got Elliot's attention, but really, he liked your book. He asked me all kinds of questions about it. Mostly if all those things really happened and I told him yes. That was when he said we had to have you on the show. Next Tuesday. Please?"

I got over my modesty and agreed. Somebody who didn't even know me liked my book. And I was going to be on TV.

We finished a very nice dinner, went home and Tangee stuck a smiley face on the calendar and drew an exclamation mark next to it. Later, she even let me shower in the big bathroom, but then I had to go to my hut.

I woke up the next morning thinking about Tuesday. What would I wear? What would I say? What kind of questions was she going to ask? When I left work I stopped off at my brother Roy's house to ask him.

"That's great," said Roy. "Lots of people watch Tangee's show. I'll bet you sell a lot of books."

"But what am I going to do? Or say or wear? What if she asks me things I can't answer? I don't even know for sure that she's read it."

"Man. You don't even know if she's read it? You're still doing that hut thing?"

"Yeah."

"I read the copy you gave me. It's good. Funny. Kind of short, though. And when I got to the end, I thought there should have been more of an ending. I mean, you get back from your trip to Las Vegas and you have your fireworks and then it's over. It could have used more of an ending."

"Like what?" I asked. "It ended the way it ended. I told the story of the BaitKing party and the Vegas trip. That's what I wanted to write about and when the stories were over, the book was done."

"Hmm." Said Roy. "Sure. It's your book. And I liked it. And you're worried what you're going to wear?"

"I had my suit cleaned, but suits are mostly for funerals and weddings. And I have a few good sport coats, but maybe they're too casual. I don't know."

"Navy blazer," said Roy. "Can't fail with a navy blazer and gray slacks. Perfect for everything. And a light blue shirt. I think light blue shirts photograph well for TV."

"A tie?"

"I'm not sure. Tell you what, carry a tie in your pocket and if they say where's your tie, you pull it out." Roy is smart. Then he said, "Now, about your living in your hut…"

"I know. It's stupid," I said. "But she still hasn't come around. I thought for sure by now she'd give it up."

"Why?"

"Huh?"

"Why would she give it up? In fact, why is she doing it in the first place?"

"You know. There's this Doctor Franklin Pewamic…"

"No," Roy interrupted. "This is not about Doctor Pewamic. Why is Tangee doing this? She has her own reasons that have nothing to do with the doctor. That book was just a little push to do something she already had in mind."

"What are you talking about? Nothing had happened until that book happened. Everything had been fine. Sure, Tangee had her new job, but I let her do that. I never stood in her way. She could do what she wanted. I didn't pay much attention."

"Think about that," said Roy. Then, before I could say anything he got up and said, "I'm going to take a shower. Go home and dust off your navy blazer."

I did just that. I went home and took my navy blazer out of its filmy, plastic dry cleaner bag and found a tie to match. I hung them up to wait for Tuesday.

Before I went to bed I thought about what Roy had said and decided he didn't know much about Tangee or Doctor Pewamic.

It took a long time for Tuesday to come.

Tangee usually taped her shows. Then, every night, she'd sit at the anchor desk and when they turned the show over to her, she'd talk for a second about what her segment was going to be about. Then she led into a commercial and when the commercial was over, the tape she'd made earlier in the day would play. For one reason or another we weren't able to tape our segment and it was decided that she would interview me live.

I sat in a burgundy chair. Next to me was a small table and on the other side of the table, a second burgundy chair. This was Tangee's interview set. It was apart from the regular news set where the anchors had their desks. Behind a glass partition was the control room, but I couldn't see much of what was going on in there. Elliot Schurmer was reading a story about last quarter's auto production. When they went to a taped segment by a reporter, Tangee looked over at me and waved.

She looked great, wearing a dark blue silk blouse and cream colored slacks. I had watched earlier as she walked around the set before the show. She seemed to move different than she did at home or anywhere else. She looked taller.

They had told me that after the regular news and weather and sports, they would turn the show over to her. She'd do a tease; a short introduction of what the viewers could expect after the commercial. Then she would have to scoot over the second burgundy chair and wait for her cue. I had wanted to rehearse some of the questions she'd be asking me, but she said it would be better if we didn't. The interview would be fresher that way, she said. She told me not to worry because she wouldn't be asking any tricky questions. Everything would be very smooth and natural. There was a coffee mug of water for me on the little table, and I wanted a sip, but I figured that I was nervous enough already and didn't want to find myself needing to take a piss halfway through our talk.

I sat through the news and got a little itchy during the weather report and by the time the sports report was on, I was squirming. I couldn't remember how to sit. No position felt right. I crossed my legs one way and then the other but that didn't help. I wondered what to do with my hands and tried folding them in my lap and then resting them on the arms of the chair. They didn't seem to belong anywhere.

And then Tangee was talking into the camera and looking fresh and new but still just like always. Her voice was still her voice but somehow it was clearer. A commercial came on and the lights came up on the interview set. Tangee started walking over to me.

Then something happened. As she walked, I saw her in her blue top and cream colored slacks, but somehow I also saw her in jeans and a tee shirt and in that black dress she wears to weddings and in that pair of shorts she wears when she's working in the garden. I saw it all at once, kind of like a mirage.

She sat down and I think she told me how many seconds it would be until the commercial would be over. But I didn't exactly hear her right. My ears were ringing and her voice seemed to echo.

In those few words I heard her talk and laugh that little laugh she does when something cute surprises her. It was like I was seeing and hearing every Tangee I'd ever known, through all the years we'd been married.

The director counted down the seconds and then pointed to Tangee.

"Welcome back," she began. "I'm her with a little surprise today. I'm going to interview the author of this book." She held up a copy. "Not only is it a wonderful, funny book, but also the writer is local. And one more thing that I can be especially proud of is that he's my husband, Buck Crimmins. Welcome Buck."

It took a second to figure out the right thing to say. "Thank you," I answered.

Tangee said, "The title of the book is, 'Buck and Tangee; Things That Happen.' What kinds of things, Buck? Surly you didn't go and tell everybody all of our little secrets?"

"No," I said. "It's just a book with a couple of chapters in it. One of them is about the time we tried to sell a bunch of fishing rods and things to our friends. It didn't turn out too well." It sounded so stupid. A book with two chapters. And one of them about selling fishing rods. Who could possibly care about that? Why would I even ever bothered to write about such a thing?

"Oh, now Buck, that first chapter has a lot more to it than that. There are wonderfully funny descriptions of the crazy antics you and Roy went through that summer." She looked toward the camera, "Roy is my brother-in-law. Why don't you tell us a little about how you got the idea in the first place?"

"You mean about your PlasticQueen party?" I said. She nodded.

I started talking and a couple of minutes later I could see the woman behind one of the cameras smiling and nodding her head. I guess I described it okay.

Tangee spoke to the camera again, "When we come back I think we'll ask Mr. Crimmins to read a bit from one of the funniest sections."

"You're doing so well!" said Tangee after they went to commercial. "But try to relax a bit. I know you must be nervous, but you look like your mind is totally somewhere else."

She was right. My brain was going a million miles an hour and none of it had to do with being nervous. I was seeing things and hearing things and mostly I was thinking things. So suddenly I was all aware of how Tangee looked and sounded the day she told me she got the job at the station. It was like the last year was all of a sudden playing itself through me, but I was seeing it all for the first time. I could see her growing into her new experiences. I could see me not growing at all, except that now I was writing. Here we were on this TV set and she's interviewing me like I'm some great author when it was really her who ought to be getting interviewed for everything she had done and become. I was still in a kind of daze when I realized that Tangee was asking me another question.

"…about your trip to Las Vegas with your friends. How did you ever manage to remember all of those details?"

I thought quickly and told her and the camera just what I'd told Clement when he asked me the same question; that it was like watching a movie, and I just put down on paper what it was I saw. Tangee nodded thoughtfully.

"And the dialog in your book…would you say it's about the same with that? That you can actually hear the conversations in your head? Like listening to a tape recorder?"

"Yeah," I said. "Exactly like that." She understood.

"Buck, would you read a portion of that chapter to us? I have one picked out that shows how you handle dialog."

She handed me the book, opened to the place where I met Robert and Lori at the Alternative Lifestyles Convention in Las Vegas. I took a breath and read. When I saw my words in the book, it was like seeing an old friend. As I read it out loud I felt calm and happy and the words came out of my mouth just like I was telling the story at the Beer Bar or someplace. When I finished the passage I looked up and saw the woman at the camera holding her hand over her mouth to keep from laughing. I felt great.

Tangee said thank you to me and I felt a click in my brain. She asked me how I felt about having finished the book. I said, "It's not finished." She looked at me funny.

"There's one more chapter to go," I said.

"But, I thought you were through. Why a third chapter? What would it be about?"

"The last chapter will be about a man who took his wife for granted. It will be about a man who was so foolish that he couldn't even see how his wife was growing and making all kinds of changes in herself…changes for the good. It will be about how damn lucky he was to catch himself and all of a sudden see his wife and his marriage in a whole new way. I hope at the end of that last chapter, his wife forgives him for being such a jerk. If the book doesn't have that as a last chapter, it's all kind of a waste."

Tangee actually had a tear in her eye. She said, "The man in the last chapter wasn't a jerk. At least not all the time. And his wife did some silly things too. And if he'll forgive her, she'll forgive him."

I just nodded.

Tangee said to the camera, "See, I told you he was a great writer. I love happy endings. But, I guess you'll have to wait a little while to buy this book. The author still has some work to do." Then she took a breath as the director counted down to the end of the show. "This is Tangee Crimmins. Thanks for watching." A commercial came on and Tangee was in my lap. We kissed and said lots of things to each other that I'm not going to write here. Then we walked to the TV station's lunchroom and talked some more.

We sat on the molded plastic chairs and talked about lots of things that should have been talked about many months before. I said, "You read my book."

Tangee nodded, "Well of course I read your book. The first time I read the whole thing all the way through was just after Willoughby delivered them all printed up, but I read parts of it a couple of times before that."

"When?" I asked.

"Well, you left a part of it for me to read in an envelope one time. I was surprised you didn't come right out and ask me what I thought of it."

"I asked you what you thought of my manuscript, didn't I?"

"Yes, and I wrote you back, too."

"You said my manuscript was hard to read."

"Bucky, your handwriting has always been terrible." I laughed and Tangee looked like she wanted to laugh too. I told her the difference between the words "manuscript" and "handwriting." But I was very careful not to sound like I was talking down to her. I guessed I'd done too much of that already.

After we'd talked for a while a fellow came into the room holding a phone. "Call for you, Tangee."

She shook her head, "Not now."

"I think you want to take this call," he said.

She took the phone. "Yes, this is Tangee Crimmins. Good. I'm glad you enjoyed it. Well, actually he's still here, do you want to talk to him?"

She handed me the phone. "Hello?" I said.

The caller was Rachel Stern. She was a literary agent and she'd seen the show. She said that when I finished my new last chapter I should send her the book. She was positive that she could find a real publisher for me. I was amazed.

Then what happened was that I did write the new last chapter and I did send it all to her and she did find a publisher. Right now we're waiting to hear if the publisher is interested, but I guess if you're reading this now, they were. So anyway, that's all I have to write for now. Thanks for buying my book and I hope you liked it.

About the author:

Jon Zech has been writing for over fifty years, but has only seriously begun submitting for publication in the last few years. Most recently, he has earned an award in Glimmer Train, and won the Springfed Arts 2012 Fiction contest. He is currently in Short Story America's Anthology, Volume II. His story, "A Short, Good Ride," is scheduled for publication in Echo Ink Review in the fall of 2012.

He lives near Anchor Bay, Michigan, with his wife and various dachshunds.

About Woodward Press:

Woodward Press LLC is a southeast Michigan company that publishes literary novels and short story collections. Our Woodweird Press division publishes speculative fiction, including horror, science fiction, fantasy, magical realism, slipstream and steampunk. Our web site is http://woodwardpress.com.